Waking the Qi:

An Introduction to Qigong

By John Munro

Disclaimer

No part of this book is intended as medical advice, or to be used as a substitute for appropriate medical care.

Neither this nor any other exercise program should be followed without first consulting a health care professional. If you have any special conditions requiring attention, you should consult with your health care professional regarding the suitability of the exercises and practices contained in this book and possible modifications.

The author and publisher are not liable for any damage, injury or other adverse outcome resulting from the application of information contained in this book.

ISBN-13: 978-1541197299

Printed by CreateSpace, An Amazon.com Company
Available from Amazon.com and other retail outlets

Foreword

I have written this book with the aim of providing the interested student or enthusiast with a simple and practical guide to begin their journey into the wide world of qigong.

At its core qigong is about 'qi', living vital life-force energy. Learning to become aware of it, feel it, sense it, direct it, and work with it. For various reasons this 'qi' can become inactive in people, like going to sleep. This can be due to stress, injury, ill health, long periods of inactivity and other factors. When this happens, the energy withdraws to the centre and it is much harder to identify and feel its flow through the body.

The exercises you will learn in this book are designed to gently wake up your 'qi' or life force energy and activate its flow within your body. When the qi flows it brings health strength and vitality to your whole being. When your qi is awakened you will find it easier to feel this energy in other qigong practices or energy arts that you are already involved in. They will become more powerful and effective as there is more energy, more vital life-force, available to be directed in these practices.

If all of this sounds a bit mysterious to you, read on... Each exercise is explained in terms of the role of Mind, Body, and Breath, and how these combine to create the exercise's effect. It is hoped that by presenting this practical analysis of these exercises that students will take this same practical approach to studying and understanding other qigong practices that they may encounter, and help them to deepen their understanding and make the practices less of a mystery and more of a practical and useful tool for achieving health, vitality, and wellbeing.

If you have read my previous book 'Qigong Foundation Practices' published in 2008, you may recall that at the end of that book there was reference to a series of future books on a variety of other qigong subjects. Well the future has finally arrived! This book 'Waking the Qi' is the first in a series of new books which will provide instructions and information about a wide range of qigong practices. These books will provide additional information and theory about the different practices that have been available to learn through the Long White Cloud Qigong website for some time, and other practices as well.

In reviewing the different practices and people's experience in learning them, it has been recognized that while the twelve exercises for the organ meridians presented in 'Qigong Foundation Practices' are a fascinating and useful set of exercises to learn, for many absolute beginners they can be a little complex as a starting point. For this reason you may notice some of the introductory material previously found in 'Qigong Foundation Practices' repeated here, as this book is intended to cover everything someone needs to begin their practice. Don't worry though, the vast bulk of this book is new material presenting different practices and perspectives from those found in the previous book. There will also be a new book coming out soon specifically focusing on the twelve organ meridian exercises found in 'Qigong Foundation Practices' and presenting more detailed theory and analysis of the exercises for the benefit of interested students.

You may notice that there is a significant amount of whitespace in some parts of this book. This is intentional as the book has been laid out to be used as a reference guide for people learning and practicing the exercises in it. For this reason the pages have been laid out so that the illustrations of the exercises are found on the facing page to the instructions for those exercises wherever possible to make it easier for students to follow, and this has necessarily meant the inclusion of a certain amount of whitespace to allow this layout design.

Whether you are a new student or old, I hope that you will find this book useful and enriching to your understanding of your qigong practice.

If you need additional support or resources to help you with your practice, please refer to the website at: www.longwhitecloudqigong.com

Note on spelling and pronunciation

Qigong can be spelled many different ways (Qi gung, Chi kung, Chi kong, Chi goong etc.) Some of these different spellings have arisen due to different systems of anglicising the Chinese language historically, others due to different authors trying to phonetically come up with a spelling to represent how it sounds to them. Throughout this book we will use the spelling Qigong, as this is how it is spelled in the Pinyin system of Anglicisation. Pinyin is now the standard method of representing Chinese words using the Latin alphabet, and is used throughout all parts of China. Most modern authors use this standardised spelling to help avoid confusion, but it is helpful to know that you may come across some of these other spellings, particularly in older writing, and they are in fact referring to the same thing.

To help with pronunciation of the word qigong you can say 'Chee' (as in cheese) and 'Gong' (as in a large round metal disc that you strike to make a sound). It should be noted though, that there are different accents and dialects throughout China, and so even a native Chinese speaker will say 'qigong' differently from another native Chinese speaker depending on where they are from. So it is more important to understand the concepts that the term 'qigong' represents than to worry too much about the finer points of pronunciation.

x

Table of Contents

Disclaimer iii

Foreword...v

Note on spelling and pronunciation.....................................ix

Chapter 1: Mysterious Qi (What is Qigong?) 1

Chapter 2: Principles of Qigong Practice 5

    The Mind...5

    The Breath 7

    The Body 8

    Putting It All Together..11

Chapter 3: Establishing Your Practice 13

    Where 13

    When 15

    Why...16

    How...17

Chapter 4: Introduction to Waking the Qi 19

    The Main Benefits of the Waking The Qi Practices.........20

    Sitting Instructions..21

    Note on number of repetitions and speed of movements.............22

Chapter 5: Waking the Qi - Breathing Practices 23

    Cleaning the Furnace 25

    Kindling the flame - Bellows breathing.......................29

    Balancing Activity - Alternate Nostril breathing 33

    Breathing with the Rhythm of the Universe 37

Chapter 6: Waking the Qi - Sitting Practices........................43

Activate the Energy - Chanting and vibration 45

Bow in Humility..49

Raise Hands to Heaven 53

Survey the World Around You 57

Beat the Heavenly Drum..61

Chapter 7: Waking the Qi – Transition from Sitting to Standing 65

Turning the Centre..67

Extending The Legs To The Rear 71

Extending The Legs To The Front..77

Chapter 8: Waking the Qi - Standing Practices 82

Rise and Fall 83

Bounding Leopard (Breathing Squat) 87

Eagle Spreads It's Wings and Soars...91

Dragon Spies It's Prey 95

Stir the Clouds..99

Thunder 103

Lightning 107

Standing in the Rain...111

Chapter 9: Awareness of Energy...115

Rubbing Hands...116

Clapping 117

Feel the Field 118

Cycling..119

Pulling and Pushing...120

Forming a Ball 121

Qi Storage 122

Sensations of Energy..124

Chapter 10: A Wide World of Qigong to Explore................125

Chapter 11: FAQs..128

Isn't Qigong just for old people? 128

Qigong Is 'Internal', it works only on the energy. It can't give you a beautiful body like other types of exercise can it? 128

What is the difference between Qigong and Taiji (also spelt Tai Chi)?..129

What is the difference between Qigong and Yoga? 129

Are there any restrictions on doing Qigong?.....................130

Why is Qigong so slow? 130

Is Qigong some kind of martial art?.............................131

Is Qigong Chinese?...131

I have seen two different people do the same Qigong exercise differently from one another. Is one right and the other wrong? 132

How many styles of Qigong are there?............................132

If there are so many styles of qigong, how can I find what is right for me? 133

What is Qi?..133

Is Qigong a type of Religion (or superstition)? 133

Is Qigong Dangerous? 134

Can Qigong give me super powers? 134

What science is there to support the effectiveness of Qigong? 135

Why haven't I heard of Qigong before? 135

Why don't more hospitals and medical clinics use qigong if it is 135

so effective?..135

If I do Qigong I don't need to go to the doctor, right?............136

Can Qigong make me immortal?.................................136

I have heard that Qigong includes sexual practices, is this true?
....136

Does attaining mastery in qigong equate to a higher level of
morality?...137

I have heard that Qigong will take a lifetime to learn?.............137

Is Qigong an ancient art?...138

Where did qigong come from?.....................................138

I've heard people talk about 'lineage' when discussing qigong and
martial arts. What are they talking about, and is this important?
....139

What is the relationship between Qigong and creativity?........139

Is there such a thing as too much qigong?.....................140

If I do qigong do I still need to do other types of exercise?.......140

What is the message of qigong?.................................141

Can qigong cure my...?...141

Is there some kind of special diet for qigong?..................142

About the author 143

Chapter 1: Mysterious Qi (What is Qigong?)

What imagery comes to mind when you think of qigong? Is it martial arts masters doing amazing feats of agility, strength, and resilience? (think running up walls, having bricks broken on them, balancing on the tips of spears, and so on). Or maybe an old medicine man healing sickness and injury by holding and moving his or her hands above the patient's body without even touching it! Perhaps the imagery that comes to mind is of monks in robes sitting in their lofty monasteries meditating and pondering the mysteries of life. Or it could be that you just think of a group of old people doing gentle exercises in a park. What could all these things possibly have in common?

What runs through them all is an understanding of this mysterious 'qi' or living energy. Historically martial artists found that developing this 'qi' energy made them stronger, faster, more resilient and gave them the advantage over their opponents. Doctors and healers found that by understanding and harnessing this energy they were able to heal their patients of ailments that would not respond to other treatments. They also found that they could use various practices to maintain their own health and recommend these to their patients to help them to heal themselves. Monks and those following a spiritual path found that working with this energy was a key to gaining insight and understanding of their place in the universe. Nowadays older people have discovered the benefits of qigong in helping them to maintain their health and vitality and recovering from illness. For this reason it has become very popular with this demographic in China, and it is growing in popularity around the world.

It should be noted though, that just because qigong has become popular with older people doesn't mean that it is something JUST for old people. People of all ages can benefit from qigong in the same ways that people did historically, improving physical performance like the martial artist, health and longevity like the healer and their patients, and understanding yourself and the world around you like the monk. The sooner you begin the process of learning to understand 'qi' and practice to develop skill with it, the more it will benefit you throughout your life!

So what is this 'qi' energy and why is it so mysterious?

Quite simply 'qi' is the energy of life. How would you describe the living energy in your body? It's not easy, it has many parts. There is heat from cellular metabolism, there is vibration from movement, there is electricity and magnetism from activity of the nervous system and movement of charged particles in the body and so on (this is not an exhaustive list), but no one of these by itself is 'qi'. To make things even trickier all of these different types of energy are associated with each other and convert into each other. If you rub your skin somewhere on your body, the movement will cause vibration which will stimulate the cells to be more active and generate heat, and the nerves will also become more active in response to the activity in the area... So qi is a combination of all of these things, and the qualities of it can change in many ways according to what is going on in our bodies, and also very importantly our minds as our minds drive the functioning of our bodies.

When you put all of these factors together you have something that is quite hard to describe, and even harder to measure because it is not just one thing, but a combination of many. Like most living things, it is a moving target, so in practice we often use analogies to describe it. Sometimes these analogies can sound exotic and mysterious, but they are just ways of describing many things interacting together in a way that we can grasp onto and understand without too much complexity.

Perhaps a modern analogy would help at this point.

We can think of our body like a car, and our mind like the driver. The energy or 'qi' of the car comes from the motor running, the car moving, and its interaction with the environment (such as the road or wind around it). An unskilled driver may not be able to tell much from this energy, but a skilled driver can learn to detect subtleties in the energy running through the car, like how much traction the car has with the road, whether the engine is straining and so on, and can make adjustments to how the car is being driven, maybe changing gears, or taking a different angle into a turn to give a smoother, safer, or maybe faster ride depending on the goal. The driver may also have mechanical knowledge and learn to detect subtle changes in the vibration or sound made by the car which lets the driver know of issues that need to be addressed before they become more serious. And of course, the driver can make more minor changes like adjusting the air-conditioning, turning on the stereo, or lights etc. And so the analogy continues.

Similarly with our experience of life, our bodies are always producing energy or qi, if we are unskilled we may not notice much about this energy, but when we are skilled we can tell all sorts of things about how our body is functioning and its interaction with the environment. We can make adjustments both big and small to make this functioning smoother and healthier and more effectively achieve our goals. We can also become more aware of when there is something that needs fixing in our body.

This is where the analogy of the car starts to show its limitations. You see to fix a problem with a car we would usually take it to a garage and bring in new parts to replace the old or broken ones that are

3

causing the problem. Our bodies however are much more complex than a car. They are amazing self-healing organisms, and when something needs fixing the body usually repairs or replaces/regrows the necessary parts itself. When we are skilled we can direct this to occur more effectively by directing our energy in this process.

We call this process of becoming more aware and skilled with our mind, body, and energy QIGONG, and it can help us in every area of our lives. The aim of this book is to introduce you to the fundamental principles of qigong and to help you to establish a regular practice that will set you on the path to obtaining this skill. It will teach you specific practices that 'wake up' your 'qi' to make your energy more lively and healthy and give you experience with feeling 'qi' for yourself.

While the concept of 'qi', and the amazing results that skill with 'qi' can bring, may seem mysterious to begin with, I hope that you will find the approach taken in this book decidedly non-mysterious. The why and how of each practice in this book will be explained so you can understand what it is doing in practical terms, and how it can benefit you in your life. At the end of this book there is a Frequently Asked Questions section that will help to answer many of the background questions you may have about qigong and maybe also dispel a few common qigong myths.

I hope that this book provides a valuable start on your path of self-discovery as you explore the ancient art of health and vitality: QIGONG.

Chapter 2: Principles of Qigong Practice

There are three main influences that we will work with in becoming aware of our energy and developing skill with it. Our mind, our body, and our breath. Each of these has a significant effect on the others and our energy or 'qi' is the result of the functioning of all three of these combined.

The Mind

We have already used the analogy of the mind being the driver of our 'car' – body, and it's a pretty good analogy. But we sometimes don't realise just how strong the interaction between our mind and body is and how tangible the effects of our thoughts are. It is common for people who are not aware to miss this connection and think that their thoughts and what is going on in their bodies are somehow separate.

The following exercise is a good way to illustrate just how strong the connection really is:

Exercise: Mind Body Connection

Sit in a relaxed position and close your eyes. Imagine you have your favourite food right in front of you (if you don't have a favourite food, just choose any tasty food you really like). This food could be something sweet, something sour, something spicy, salty, or bitter, maybe a juicy piece of fruit, a steaming bowl of tasty soup or stew, chocolate? it is up to you. In your mind's eye see the food as clearly as you can, sitting on a plate or in a bowl or however it is presented. Draw the food closer to you so you can see it even more clearly, notice its colours. Lift some of the food to your mouth, notice the smell as it sits in front of your mouth just below your nostrils. Take a mouthful of the food, chew on it and move it around your mouth, notice the texture and flavours. Swallow and feel the sensation of the food moving down your throat and into your belly.

Many people will notice while doing this exercise that their mouth begins to produce saliva ready to process the food. You may even notice warmth and activity in your belly as your body prepares for digestion. These are clear physical responses to something that only occurred in your mind. You knew there was not actually any food there, but your body made real physical changes in response to your thoughts.

I'm sure with just a little imagination you can come up with several other things that give a clear immediate physical response just by thinking about them. Other responses are more subtle but still occur.

Whatever we think about causes physical responses in our body, whether we are aware of them or not. If you are thinking about an argument you had with someone, your body will respond even if you are not aware of it. You will build tension in your muscles as your body prepares to brace to protect itself in case the imagined conflict becomes physical. Your hormone levels and organ function will also change to respond to the situation.

The same things apply in a more positive context if we think about something beneficial, maybe a relaxing holiday, or a happy experience with a loved one. Either way our body will respond to our thoughts.

This is neither a good or a bad thing, it is simply the way our minds and bodies work together. If we are aware of this we can turn it to our advantage and use our mind and body harmoniously together. In qigong we learn to tune into the sensations of our body and use our mind to direct its energy in beneficial ways to make it healthier and stronger. When we develop skill with our mind in this way our body responds by making the necessary changes to allow the energy to flow more freely.

Learning to tune into the sensations of energy in our body is a subtle thing and requires a clear and focused mind. So the first objective in working with our mind is to clear it of all unnecessary thoughts (which may be directing your body to respond in ways that are undesirable), and focus on the present reality of what is happening in your body here and now. One of the best methods for doing this is through working with the breath, which is the topic of the next section in this chapter.

The Breath

The breathing function is quite unique in that it is the only function of your internal organs that you can easily control both consciously and unconsciously. If you think about it you can quite easily breathe faster, slower, deeper, shallower, or even stop breathing (at least temporarily while you hold your breath). Yet if you don't think about it, you will continue to breathe without conscious thought, and if you are healthy your body will naturally regulate the speed and depth of breathing etc. in response to the demands on it.

This is because the inhalation and exhalation of the breath is driven by the skeletal muscles (abdominal muscles, rib muscles etc.) which are under conscious control, but the actual processing of the breath is driven by the smooth muscle of the lungs which is under unconscious control. The two co-ordinate with each other in order to fulfil this important function in the body, while other functions in the body that are under unconscious control such as the beating of the heart, the movement of the intestines and so on do not rely as strongly on the activity of consciously controlled skeletal muscles, and so are not as easily influenced consciously.

But, the function of the lungs affects the chemical processes of the rest of the body, so by consciously influencing the breath, it has a flow on effect influencing the unconscious functioning of all the rest of the organs in the body.

In this way the breath acts as kind of a gateway between the conscious and unconscious functioning of our body, and also the conscious and unconscious functioning of our mind. When we make the breath calm and steady, the body and mind become calm and steady as well. And as we develop skill with our breath we can use it to affect the quality and flow of energy within our body.

When we work with our breath as we perform different exercises, the exercise becomes not just about the functioning of the external skeletal muscles, but about the co-ordinated action of both the internal and external aspects of our bodies.

The Body

It should come as no surprise that moving the body affects the flow of energy in the body. What is interesting though is how much subtle changes in a movement in one part of the body can affect the energy in other parts of the body.

When we move one part of our body, it affects all of the rest of the body due to the change in weight distribution and also adjustment in tensions in the muscles and connective tissue required to support the movement or new body position. This creates physical forces in the body which stimulates the activity of cells, puts pressure on or takes pressure off nerves and blood vessels, and affects the circulation of fluids within the body.

In qigong we learn to become aware of these subtle changes and use them to affect the flow of our energy and functioning of our bodies in beneficial ways.

Exercise: Directing Force With Movement

Stand completely relaxed. Give your body a good shake, all the way through your arms, torso, legs, head, and neck, so that your body is very loose. Try letting your body sway side to side, front and back with everything very loose and relaxed.

Try raising your arm out to your side with your body loose and relaxed like this. The laws of the universe (and basic physics) tells us that for every action there has to be an equal and opposite reaction, for every force an equal and opposite force in order for the universe to stay in balance. So as you raise your arm to the side there has to be equal and opposite movement or force to balance this. If your body is completely relaxed and loose it will move in the opposite direction to the arm in order to balance its movement. So as you raise your arm to the side in one direction – your body will sway in the opposite direction. If you move your other arm to the side in the other direction, your body will move the other way. You can also try doing this by moving your arms forwards and backwards.

Notice that as you raise your arm and sway it gently affects all the tissues of your body all the way down to your feet, not just your arm.

Now try doing the same thing keeping your body still and not allowing it to sway. Notice that you can still raise your arm to the side or front and back without your body swaying. Instead your body balances this force by building tension in the body, again all the way through the torso and down the legs to the feet.

Try alternating between keeping your body still and letting it sway as you raise and lower your arms to get a sense of the difference between these two ways that your body balances the forces created by the movement.

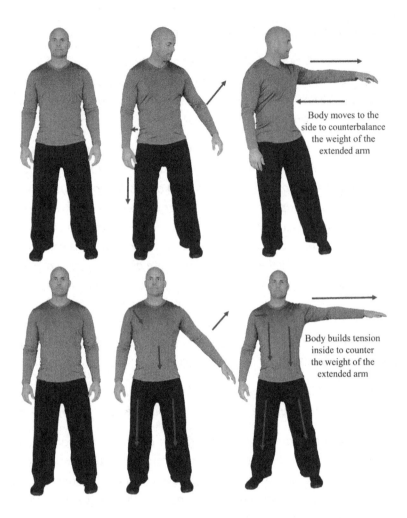

Body moves to the side to counterbalance the weight of the extended arm

Body builds tension inside to counter the weight of the extended arm

This is a very simple exercise to become aware of how the forces through your body are connected. In qigong practice we learn to make subtle adjustments to our body position and movement so that we can direct the energy of these forces in ways that are useful to us and keep our bodies healthy and strong. We also develop awareness so that we can know when we are allowing forces to move through us in ways that are harmful to us and make changes in the way we use our bodies to prevent this.

Putting It All Together

One of the powerful things about qigong practice is that we learn to work with all three of these elements together. The mind, body and breath are all involved in each practice, and the influence and effect of each is considered. In some practices the immediate attention is more on one of them than the others and is therefore 'driving' the action more, but all three are considered and affected.

As you go through the qigong practices in this book, you will find not just directions on how to do each exercise, but also a description of how each element of the mind, body and breath is engaged in the exercise, and the overall effect and benefit we are seeking to obtain when we do the practice correctly.

Chapter 3: Establishing Your Practice

Before we look at the What of the qigong practices for 'waking your qi' that you will learn in this book, it is a good idea to consider the Where, When, Why, and How of your qigong practice. One of the biggest factors in success in qigong is consistency. If you address each of the Where, When, Why, and How, you eliminate many of the common obstacles that get in the way of successful qigong practice. You will then be on the path to turn mastery of your mind, body, breath, and energy from fanciful wish to living reality.

Where

Deciding on a suitable place is an important first step in establishing your qigong practice. There are several factors to consider in choosing a location

Distractions

Tuning in to your mind and body can be a challenge to begin with. It helps when you are just beginning your practice to find somewhere with as few distractions as possible to make it easier for you to focus uninterrupted. This means finding somewhere that people are unlikely to interrupt you too often, and also considering things like how much visual and aural distraction there is in the area. Finding somewhere that there are not too many things moving around in your field of view and not too many loud or sudden noises will help you to be able to relax and focus effectively on your practice.

Environmental Energy

The quality of the energy in your environment will make a big difference to how energised you feel from your practice. Being out in nature is ideal if you can be. Practicing near lakes, rivers, the ocean, trees, mountains, and even the sun and the moon each confer different benefits to your energy that you will become more aware of as you progress in your qigong practice.

Indoors you should also consider the quality of the energy around you, clutter, dust, mould or mildew, lots of electronic devices, all these things can have a negative impact on the energy around you. So if you are going to practice indoors, find somewhere with good light, good airflow and an uncluttered space to practice in.

Comfort

It is important that your space is comfortable for you to practice in. If the space is too hot, too cold, too windy, too humid, too damp etc, your attention and energy will go to dealing with these things rather than to focusing on the beneficial energy within your body. Also within the 'Waking the Qi' practices there are some practices that involve lying down, others sitting, and others standing. Make sure you are comfortable doing each of these things at the location you choose.

Later in your practice you may choose to do only standing or only sitting exercises, so a space that is only comfortable for those will be fine then. But to begin with and to get the most out of these practices you will want to be comfortable in all three of these positions.

Convenience

This one trumps all the others really. If your space to practice is not convenient, you are less likely to practice regularly. You may know of a beautiful spot on a mountain where the environmental energy is wonderful, with a river flowing nearby and a forest which provides shelter from the wind and shade from excessive sun... but if it takes you a long time to get there it just will not be convenient to practice regularly. I recommend still finding these types of places and seeking them out to practice in from time to time, but it is important to have a convenient spot to practice in on a regular basis as well.

This usually means finding somewhere close to your home or your work. It could be your bedroom or living room or even your office if you are able to clear a suitable space there. Or it could be out in your garden or in a nearby park.

When

Setting a regular time to practice can help to ensure consistency. Traditionally there are certain times of day that are considered the most beneficial to practice. These are sunrise, midday, sunset, and midnight.

These times are most beneficial because the energy of our bodies reflect what is going on in the world around us. At sunrise the energy is moving from a state of restfulness (yin) to activity (yang) as the sun ascends into the sky, warms the earth, and gives light for us to do things by. At midday the energy is peak yang and we can channel this very active energy in certain practices. At sunset there is another key transition from activity (yang) to rest (yin) as the sun goes down and the earth cools and darkens. At midnight the energy is peak yin and again we can channel and use the quality of this energy in certain practices.

But in the end what matters most is that it is a time that works for you and you can keep to. Qigong practice midmorning or in the early evening well away from any of those key times of sunrise, sunset, midday and midnight, is still going to be greatly beneficial for you. Personally, I most enjoy early morning practice as working with my energy at this time sets me up for my day. Also with regard to my schedule, I know that if I do my practice early in the morning that nothing else will get in the way of me doing it as may occur at other times during the day. It happens that this also often coincides with sunrise, but what is really important is that the time works for me to keep to regularly.

What works for you and your schedule may be different from what works for me or other people. I find that for most people if they can anchor their qigong practice to something else in their schedule that does not change much, then there is a much greater chance that they will practice regularly. This could be getting up in the morning, or it could be lunchtime at work, or it could be when you get home from work, or maybe before you go to bed.

Find a time that works for you and then make your qigong practice a habit at this time.

Why

This is an interesting one to think about. Why do you want to practice qigong? I will admit that in my very early years of practice I was fascinated by what seemed like 'superpowers' that one could acquire through qigong practice. I was young and impressionable I guess. Over the years my ideas have changed a bit. I find myself more interested in 'ordinary powers' than 'superpowers'. Through my qigong practice I have developed abilities that to some people may seem unusual, but through understanding these are no longer particularly impressive to me, they are just like any other skill developed through time and effort, and I now find myself more interested in simply being healthy and happy.

What would you like to achieve from your qigong practice? Maybe you would like a calmer clearer mind and the ability to focus more easily? Maybe you would like to be able to move more easily and with less aches and pains? Maybe you would like to be able to understand yourself and your mental and emotional states better? Or perhaps you want to have a clearer perspective on the wonders of the universe and your place in it?

Qigong can help you to achieve all of these things and more. If you keep in mind why you are practicing qigong, it will be easier to judge for yourself whether you are getting the benefits you seek, and it will be easier for you to motivate yourself to continue to practice regularly.

Many of these benefits come slowly, little by little. So you need to remain consistent and dedicated to achieve them.

How

This largely comes down to attitude, which will flow out of your why. It is important to practice your qigong with persistence, patience, and care for yourself. Never force yourself in any of the movements or exercises. It is normal to sometimes feel some discomfort when you are doing something new, and even some aches, but if you feel any sudden sharp pains or more than mild discomfort that persists, you should stop what you are doing and seek expert advice. You may have a condition that makes certain movements unsuitable, or you may need to modify some practices in some way to make them work for you.

Pushing through pain and more than mild discomfort instead of being beneficial to you can be harmful, which will not help you to achieve your goals, but instead take you further away from them.

There is an old saying about exercise that you may have heard before, "No pain, no gain". Many of us now know that this is not true, but I like to put a little twist on that saying to make it useful to us. My version of it says "No pleasure, no gain". Qigong should feel good! And you should feel good after doing it. If you don't, you might be doing something wrong.

Similarly with your mind. If you find yourself getting distracted a lot during your qigong practice sessions, you may need to consider the nature of the distractions. Some distractions need your attention and they won't go away until you have attended to them. If this is the case, leave you qigong practice and go and deal with them. You can come back to your practice later, or even the next day, or next week. When you have dealt with the distraction you will be able to clear your mind and focus more easily. Other distractions can and should be put aside. Once you have decided that the distraction is something that does not need to be attended to right now, don't be too concerned if it keeps interrupting your focus to begin with. This is often referred to as the 'monkey mind' easily distracted and jumping from one thing to another. Harsh judgement and 'punishment' of yourself for being distracted will not help. The monkey mind responds best to gentle but firm redirection, each time your focus slips from your qigong practice, simply bring it back again without judgement. Over time your mind will respond to this training and will gradually become calmer and clearer and it will become easier for you to focus without unnecessary distraction.

Chapter 4: Introduction to Waking the Qi

This book contains a series of twenty qigong exercises. Each exercise by itself has significant benefits, and the effects of each one will be explained alongside the instructions for that exercise. When combined they have the effect of 'Waking the Qi' in your body, making it more lively and active.

When your qi is awake you will literally feel more alive as each cell in your body gets a healthy flow of life giving qi energy. You will find that you feel more relaxed, alert and energetic. You will be able to think more clearly and live a more vibrant and happy life.

The complete series will take between 10 and 45 minutes depending on how slowly you perform each exercise and also how many repetitions you do of each movement.

In addition to this, the series is divided into sections, and you may choose to do only one section at a time if you wish. This can be particularly useful if you are wanting to combine these exercises with other qigong practices. For example, the *Sitting Practices* and *Transition from Sitting to Standing* are great to do after completing a sitting meditation session as a way to gently bring the energy into the limbs and stand gracefully after a long period of stillness. The *Standing Practices* are a great way to make the energy lively throughout the whole body before moving into other standing qigong exercises. This will improve your awareness and sensation of energy in your body in whatever qigong exercises you do next, kind of an 'activator' for your qigong session. And of course you may find that there are some individual exercises that you particularly enjoy or that have benefits that are particularly relevant to you, in which case you may choose to practice these individual exercises by themselves.

'Waking the Qi' is useful for everyone. We all have natural cycles in our energy, moving between activity and rest, and 'Waking the Qi' is a great way to spark your energy up to a higher level after a time of restfulness, ready for further activity. Also, there are conditions that can make our qi go into a deeper and unhealthy type of sleep, in particular long periods of inactivity due to physical or mental health issues, or prolonged or intense periods of stress can cause the qi to withdraw and become inactive. For people in these situations the 'Waking the Qi' series of exercises will have a very beneficial therapeutic effect in helping them to return their energy to normal levels of activity.

The practices in this book are quite simple to learn, and there is not really much you can do to get them 'wrong', so following the illustrations in this book should be quite easy. If however you require additional resources, there are also videos available for these exercises which you can find at longwhitecloudqigong.com

The Main Benefits of the Waking The Qi Practices

Below is a list of the main overall benefits of the Waking the Qi series of qigong practices. The benefits of individual exercises will be discussed alongside the description of each exercise.

- More active and healthy digestion
- Easier breathing and increased lung capacity
- Strengthening, loosening, and balancing of the spine, from the lower back all the way up to the neck
- Reduction of stress hormone levels, and strengthening of the adrenal glands, kidneys, and entire hormonal system
- Stronger, more stable core muscles
- Greater ease of movement between sitting and standing from improved mobility in the back and legs
- Healthier immune function
- Improved peripheral blood circulation
- Increased sense of health and wellbeing through improved energy flow throughout the body

Sitting Instructions

The *Waking the Qi* series includes exercises in a seated position. It is important that you sit in an upright position that is comfortable to you so that you can get the most out these exercises. Some mild discomfort is ok and will probably ease as you continue to practice if you are not used to sitting, but if you are in a position that is painful for you or too uncomfortable, you are likely to tense and shift your body in ways that take away from the benefit of the exercises.

If you are comfortable sitting on the floor the ideal position is a kneeling position, but a cross-legged or lotus position can also work with some adaptation. You may want to put a rug or mat on the floor to act as cushioning when you sit.

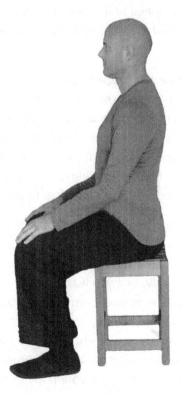

If you are not comfortable sitting on the floor, you will want a chair or a stool that you can sit on comfortably. The ideal height of this is so that your thighs are parallel to the floor when your feet rest flat on the floor. If you are using a chair you will need to sit forwards away from the back of the chair so that your spine stays upright and doesn't lean into the chair and so that your arms can move freely around your body.

Note on number of repetitions and speed of movements

As you read the information for each exercise, you will find instructions for how to do the exercises, but no set prescription of how many repetitions to do of each movement or how quickly to do them. This is because deciding on the number of repetitions to do, or the speed to do them at, is a bit like asking how long a piece of string is. It depends on the situation, what is available, and what you want it for.

How many repetitions you do of each movement and how quickly depends on several factors like, how much time do you have available? How quickly or slowly are you doing the movements? Does it feel like it would be good to do more, or does it feel like you have done enough? Do you feel like slowing, calming and relaxing, or do you feel like moving more quickly to energise and activate? In the end, how the movements feel to you should be your ultimate guide

If you do the movements very slowly with pauses between movements, you might feel quite satisfied doing each movement just once. On the other hand, if you are doing the movements more quickly, or if you want to have a longer practice session, you might do each movement ten or even more times. Qigong practice can be adapted in many ways to meet your needs. To begin with when learning, you might get into a routine of doing each exercise a certain number of times, but over time it is desirable to pay more and more attention to how your body feels and use this as the main guide in how you do your qigong practice.

Chapter 5: Waking the Qi - Breathing Practices

The first set of exercises in the *Waking the Qi* practice series are breathing exercises. You can practice these exercises on their own if you wish, or link them together with the Sitting, Transitioning From Sitting To Standing, and Standing practices, for a more comprehensive qi waking session! They are also an excellent way to start or end a seated meditation practice session.

Cleaning the Furnace

The Chinese refer to the internal organs as being part of a furnace to generate energy throughout the body. It's a pretty good analogy as eating food and then breathing and being active to burn the food eaten is quite similar to burning fuel in a furnace in many ways.

One of the things that can happen if our energy has gone to sleep is that our digestive functions deteriorate and can lead to stagnancy of the energy in the abdomen. This stagnancy then gets in the way of us burning fuel and making energy in our furnace efficiently. This particularly effects the lungs as for us to breathe efficiently our abdomen needs to be able to move freely so our diaphragm muscle can descend and rise easily allowing the filling and emptying of the lungs. Any accumulation of stagnant energy in the abdomen gets in the way of this free movement and impairs the lungs functioning. This stagnancy can take the form of muscle tension, stagnant blood, undigested food, visceral fat, or build-up of waste in the large intestine.

The following practice is designed to gently increase activity throughout the digestive system and encourage better digestion, and clearance of waste or other stagnancy, allowing the lungs to function more freely, and better overall energy production.

For some people the results of this exercise will be immediate and dramatic, for others the change may be slower, and they will notice a more gradual improvement in digestion and elimination and sense of ease in the abdomen.

Instructions

Step One: Drink a class of water with 1 tablespoon of fresh lemon juice or raw unpasteurized apple cider vinegar.

Step Two: Lie down on your back and stand your feet to relax your back. Take a normal breath in and then breathe out so that the belly falls. Hold the belly in and breathe in again so that the chest and back expands. Hold your breath and push your belly out and in as many times as you feel comfortable and then pull your tummy in and breathe out.

Step Three: Massage your abdomen with downward strokes using a comfortable pressure

Step Four: Repeat Step Two

Step Five: Massage your abdomen with circular strokes in a clockwise direction using a comfortable pressure

Step 1.

Step 2.

Take a normal breath in | Then breathe out so that your belly falls

Hold your belly in and breathe in so that your chest and back expands | Hold your breath and push your belly out

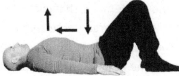 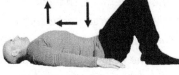 

Keep holding your breath and pull your belly back in again | Repeat as many times as is comfortable pushing your belly out and in with your breath held

Then pull your belly in and breathe out. Return to normal breathing

Step 3.   Step 5.

Mind

Our 'mind' incorporates more than just our brain. It includes all of our modes of 'thinking' and processing information. Some of this is done in our belly by our enteric nervous system. This is part of why we get 'gut feelings' about things, the information was actually processed in the gut. When there is stagnancy in the belly this interferes with the functioning of our enteric nervous system, and when we clear this stagnancy we find that all of our 'thinking' becomes more clear.

Body

The movement of the belly helps to move the water and lemon juice/cider vinegar down through the digestive system, stimulating it's cleansing and eliminative functions.

Breath

You should always aim to breathe in a way that is suitable to your activity. Most of the time this involves smooth even breathing that co-ordinates with your movements. There are a few times when that means holding the breath, and this is one of them. Pushing your belly out and in is driven by the diaphragm muscle (a large dome shaped muscle which sits up under the ribs). The diaphragm is also the muscle that is primarily responsible for powering the inhalation of the breath. So to allow our belly to move in and out quickly without interfering with our breathing, we hold our breath throughout this phase of the exercise. This exercise will also make the diaphragm muscle stronger, more flexible, and more co-ordinated, which will make it more effective for its role in breathing.

Kindling the flame - Bellows breathing

Having cleansed the furnace, it is now time to kindle the 'fire' of our digestion using a very active bellows breath, much like blowing on a flame to make it grow larger and burn hotter. Our aim in doing this is to activate the energy in our abdomen so that it feels warm, active, and glowing.

Instructions

Sit comfortably with your body upright.

Take a full deep breath in, allowing your belly to relax outwards.

Breath a short sharp breath out by squeezing in with the abdomen.

Let the abdomen naturally relax to draw air in again (put no effort into the inhalation, focus on powering the exhalation and letting the inhalation follow naturally as you relax the contraction used for the exhalation).

Repeat in a rhythmic fashion.

This breath is very fast and you will normally do quite a high number of repetitions in a short space of time. You can continue until the energy in your abdomen feels warm and glowing, or until your abdominal muscles start to fatigue.

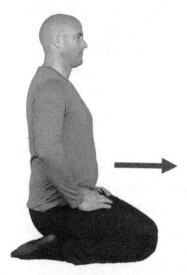

Breathe a deep breath in
allowing your belly to
relax outwards

Breathe a short sharp breath
out, causing the belly to
draw in

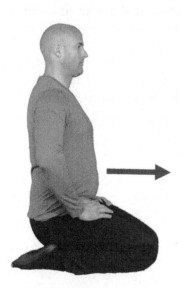

Let the lungs fill quickly and
naturally by letting the belly
relax out quickly

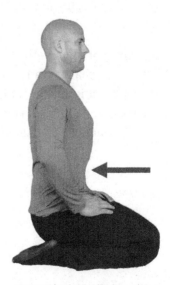

Repeat rhythmically, breathing
short sharp out breaths and
then letting the belly relax out

31

Mind

You can aid in the kindling of your inner fire by focusing on any sensations of heat or energy in your abdomen and imagining it like a flame. With each pump of your 'bellows', imagine blowing on this flame making the energy glow warmer and brighter.

Body

This rapid movement squeezing with the abdomen stimulates the digestive organs and speeds up the metabolism as the digestive fire grows stronger, increasing the energy generated. These pumping contractions also strengthen the deep abdominal muscles helping to stabilise the spine and trunk of the body, allowing physical activity and movement to be easier and more efficient.

Breath

This breathe focusing on the rapid exhalation helps to relax the diaphragm muscle as the inward contraction of the deep abdominal muscles support the diaphragm's lengthening and upward movement.

The rapid nature of the breath also helps us to broaden our range of breathing skills so that we can more easily adapt to different situations. Just as it is healthy for us to be able to breathe deep and slow to help us to relax, it is also important for us to be able to breathe shallow and quick to be efficient in very active situations.

Balancing Activity - Alternate Nostril breathing

As our energy starts to become more active and glow brighter and stronger, we need to make sure that it is balanced throughout our body. Without realising it we can sometimes have one side of our body more active than the other. The left side of our brain is primarily responsible for movement and muscle activation in the right side of our body, and the right side of our brain is primarily responsible for the left side of the body.

The breath through our nostrils has an important role in stimulating the activity of our brain. When we breathe through one nostril more than the other, it activates one side of our brain more than the other. By practicing alternating breathing through each nostril, we balance this activity in our brain and body. This then balances the energy generation and activity in the rest of our body as well.

Instructions

Sit comfortably as before.

Place the index and middle finger of one hand between your eyebrows.

Cover one nostril with your thumb, breathe in. Release your thumb and cover the other nostril with your ring finger, breathe out. Keep this nostril covered with your ring finger and breathe in. Release your ring finger and cover the other nostril with your thumb, breathe out. This is one cycle.

Repeat for several cycles.

If you find that one nostril is more blocked than the other and is difficult to breathe through, don't be too concerned. Continue to practice and over several sessions this will become easier.

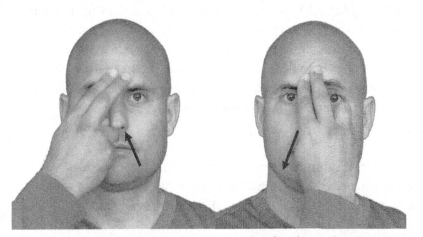

Cover one nostril with your
thumb and breathe in

Switch and cover the other
nostril with your ring finger
and breathe out

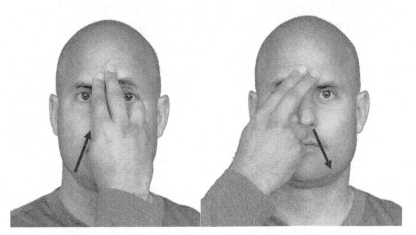

Keep the same nostril covered
and breathe in again

Switch and cover you other
nostril with your thumb
and breathe out

Repeat for several full rounds

Mind

The left side of the brain is associated with logical thinking, the right side is associated with creativity. Sometimes we can become stuck using one or the other. Ideally we want to be able to use both equally well and move between them easily as needed. Breathing in this way can help to alternate the activity between each side of the brain and can help to balance out your thinking habits.

Body

The effect is subtle, but breathing in this way will affect the nerve activation in each side of the body, which can help to correct a situation where there is weakness in one side of the body.

Breath

As you practice this breathing it will become easier for your body to open each side of your sinuses when you need to, making difficulty breathing through the nose due to blocked sinuses less common.

Breathing with the Rhythm of the Universe

The next exercise is to practice taking deep full breaths using what is known as the rhythm of the universe. This rhythm is harmonious with the natural rhythms of nature and when we breath in this rhythm both our mind and body become calm and balanced. When our breathing becomes slower it will also naturally become deeper and encourages us to relax and lengthen all of the different muscles used in breathing, helping us to stretch out and loosen the 'furnace' of our abdomen used for energy production.

Instructions

Sit in a comfortable position. This can be kneeling, cross legged, or in a chair. Keep your body relaxed and upright.

Inhale slowly for a count of eight, pause for four, exhale slowing for a count of eight, pause for four and then repeat.

Do as many repetitions as you wish.

The expansion of the breath should begin in your abdomen and then gently rise upwards to your ribs and shoulders as you inhale, and then contract back inwards and downwards in reverse order.

If you find it too difficult to breath this slowly, start with a faster rhythm of the same proportion, perhaps 4:2:4:2, then you can lengthen this to 6:3:6:3, and eventually 8:4:8:4

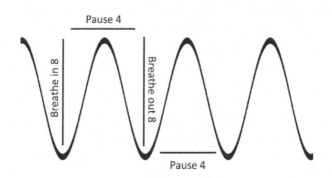

Mind

There is a strong relationship between the speed at which we breathe and the state of our mind. In general, the faster we breath the more active and stimulated our mind will be. The slower we breathe the calmer we become. There are limits to this though and the rhythm of the universe is the lower safe limit and an ideal way to breathe to put yourself in a state of calm that will allow you to be mindful and aware of the energy sensations in your body. Breathing more slowly than this can be useful in advanced practice but there are risks associated (physical and psychological) and this should only be done with expert guidance and supervision.

Body

As already mentioned breathing slowly naturally tends to also mean breathing more deeply so that we process enough volume of air during the length of the breath. This stretches and lengthens the breathing muscles. Breathing slowly also helps to co-ordinate the action of the muscles involved in breathing, meaning they will be able to work together more efficiently when they need to move quickly or under load.

Breath

Breathing deep full breaths not only increases the size of our inhalation, but also encourages us to breathe out more fully to exhale stale gases allowing us to take in more fresh clean air when we inhale again. In this way breathing deeply and slowly with the rhythm of the universe acts as a way of cleansing out the stale gases from our lungs.

More On Breathing...

Breathing is a fascinating subject that affects every area of our lives and wellbeing. This section of the book has given brief instructions on these few breathing exercises that form part of the *Waking the Qi* series of practices. These are a great place to get started!

If you would like to understand your breathing better and develop more skill with it, *Release The Power of Your Breath* by Long White Cloud Qigong contains more detailed information about the exercises you have experienced in this book and many others as well. See *Chapter 10: A Wide World of Qigong to Explore*, for where to find out more about this and other aspects of qigong practice.

Chapter 6: Waking the Qi - Sitting Practices

These sitting practices are an excellent way to end a breathing exercise session or seated meditation session, gently waking the energy in the body before rising and continuing with other activities. It has particular benefits for the spine as it activates and cares for each section of the muscles attaching to the spine in sequence, encouraging healthy movement. It also has particular benefits for the hormonal system through the activation of the kidneys, and all of the nervous system and brain as the practices bring energy up from the base of the spine to the head and face.

Activate the Energy - Chanting and vibration

Sound has a particular ability to penetrate through every part of our being. As the sound waves pass through us we can use these vibrations to activate the energy of every cell of our body as the cells literally move back and forth in response to the vibrations.

This can be harnessed through the practice of chanting. Our body needs to brace and vibrate differently to make different sounds, so different sounds have different effects on our body and energy. In our *Waking the Qi* practice we will use the sound 'Om'. This sound is commonly used in many practices for good reason as it is well balanced and has a gentle calming and cleansing effect. It is great for general purpose use activating and balancing the energy.

Instructions

Sit in a comfortable position. Breathe a full deep breath in, pause and then make the sound 'Om', make this sound as long and even as you comfortably can.

Repeat several times

Many people feel self-conscious about chanting to begin with, even when they are by themselves. I find that it really helps if you tune in to the sensation of the vibration caused by the sound more than to the sound itself. This takes your mind off what you <u>sound</u> like, and puts it more onto what the chanting <u>feels</u> like.

Focus on the sensation of vibration more
than on what it sounds like

Mind

Sometimes our mind can be noisy as we think about different things. When we tune in to the vibration of the sound as we chant, this vibration clears away all the other sounds leaving our mind particularly clear and quiet when we finish.

Body

The vibration from the sound penetrates our whole body, subtly stimulating every cell, and helping to gently move parts of our body that have become 'stuck' in position and may not respond to more overt efforts to move them. Once they start to move a little with the vibration of the sound it becomes easier for them to move more freely in response to other stimuli.

Breath

To make a long even chanting sound our breath needs to also be steady and even. Chanting is one way we learn to support our movement with our breath.

Bow in Humility

The first movement in our sitting sequence is a bowing movement. This does not have to have any kind of religious connotation unless you want it to. The movement has significant physical benefits particularly focused on the lower back which will be described in the exercise description.

Instructions

Sit comfortably with hands resting one above the other in your lap with palms facing upwards, body upright

Breathe in, in preparation to begin the movement.

Breathe out, reach your hands out in front of you on the ground. Bend forwards and place your forehead on the ground or on the backs of your hands.

Breathe in, sit back up.

Repeat several times.

(If you are sitting in a chair, reach your hands forwards down your legs as far as you can go instead of directly on the ground, and of course your head will not reach the ground, just bend as far forwards as you comfortably can).

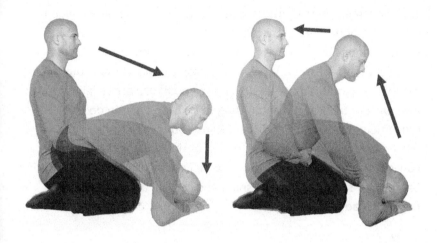

Bowing when sitting on the ground

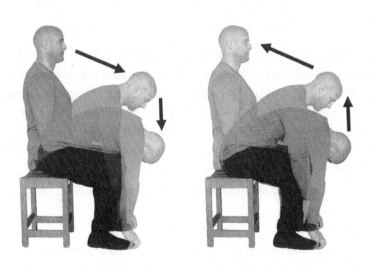

This exercise can be easily adapted for
sitting on a stool or chair

51

Mind

This movement puts us into a submissive posture. Someone who is proud or stubborn will generally not 'bow down'. Practicing this movement encourages the mind to be more humble and ready to submit when necessary. What you choose to submit to in your mind as you perform this movement is up to you. If you are religious you may wish to think about submitting to your God as you do this movement, but equally you could think about submitting to the universe, to wisdom, your higher self, or the higher good if these concepts are more comfortable to you. Equally important is the sitting back up, re-straightening the spine and coming back to an upright position ready for activity.

Body

If we become too braced in an upright position this can lead to stiffness and pain particularly in the lower back. When we bend the back, and bow forwards we need to relax and lengthen the muscles of the lower back in order to do this.

Equally if the muscles of our lower back have been too loose for too long, this can lead to the posture in the lower back collapsing and not supporting the rest of the spine and body properly. Lifting the body up from the bowing position activates and strengthens the lower back muscles as they contract to bring the body and spine upright again. This alternating movement between lengthening and then contracting the muscles of the lower back encourages blood flow to these muscles and makes them stronger and more flexible.

Breath

If our belly becomes too big, it can get in the way of the abdominal muscles drawing in effectively to support the upward movement of the diaphragm during the exhalation. Bending forwards into the bowing position naturally pushes the belly inwards and supports this upward movement and more complete relaxation of the diaphragm.

Raise Hands to Heaven

This exercise brings the focus of the movement and energy up higher to the mid back and ribs. Similar to the last exercise it also has significant psychological associations which you could choose to think of in either religious terms or more generally according to your personal preferences and beliefs.

Instructions

Sit comfortably with hands resting one above the other in your lap with palms facing upwards, body upright

Breathe in, in preparation to begin the movement.

Breathe out, extend arms out to the sides of the body at shoulder height. Palms facing outwards and fingers pointing up.

Breathe in, Rotate the arms so that the fingertips face down and raise the arms up until the heels of the hands touch above the head, look up.

Breathe out, lower the arms to the sides to shoulder height with the fingertips facing up.

Repeat the last two movements several times.

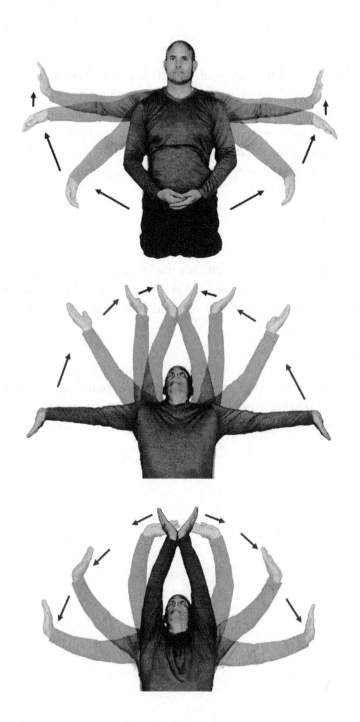

Mind

As you raise your hands and look up, this is a natural posture of praise, gratitude, or supplication. You can take the opportunity as you do this movement to have an attitude of gratitude and give praise for those good things you have in your life. You may also take the opportunity to think about those good things you wish to receive in your life. This then influences the quality of your energy subtly throughout the rest of your activities.

Body

This movement lengthens the muscles which connect from the arms down into the mid-back, specifically the latissimus dorsi muscle. Activating and moving the muscles in this way makes them healthier and stronger and encourages the shoulders to sit wider and more evenly on top of the spine.

Breath

Breathing in as the arms raise over the head stretches and expands the ribcage, making expansion with the ribs while breathing during other movements easier.

Survey the World Around You

Having bowed in humility and given thanks, praise, and supplication, you are now ready to look at the world around you with fresh eyes.

Instructions

With your arms at shoulder height and extended to the sides with the palms facing outwards and the fingers pointing up, turn your head side to side, first looking at your hand, then looking beyond your hand, and then back at your hand again on each side.

Repeat several times.

Breathe naturally throughout this exercise.

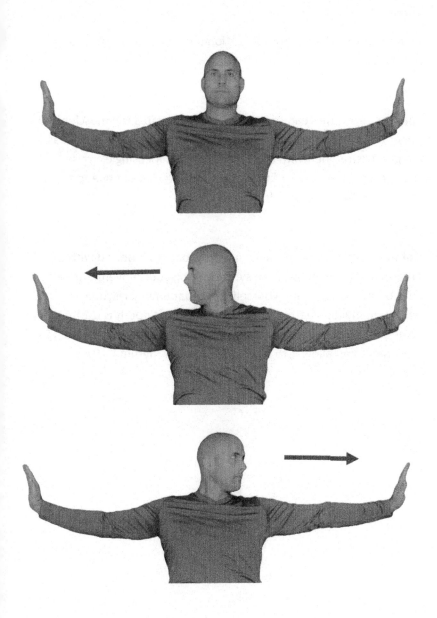

Mind

In this exercise we send our attention outwards to see the world around us

Body

The turning of the head from side to side activates the muscles in the upper back (trapezius muscle) and also the muscles in the neck as they are gently stretched with the turn. It is also a focusing exercise to strengthen the muscles of the eyes as we alternate between focusing on our hand and focusing further away.

Breath

Not every movement we make needs to be synchronised with the breath. If you always practice synchronising your movements with your breath you can find yourself in a situation where you only breath when you move, whether this is appropriate or not. It is useful to have some practices where you consciously uncouple the breath from the movement and allow it to function at its own rhythm

Beat the Heavenly Drum

There are several different exercises which bear this name. Their commonality is that they involve stimulating the nerves of the spinal cord and the brain through some type of beating of drumming action, although this is applied in different ways in different versions of this practice. In this version we will not only use a beating action but we will also follow this up with other types of physical and energy massage. The overall effect is to strengthen the kidneys and cause energy to rise up through the spinal cord to nourish the brain.

Instructions

Sit in a comfortable position and bring the hands behind the back and strike each side of the spine in the lower back area with loose fists in a rhythmic fashion. Move the hands up and down the back, beating in this way.

Raise the arms to the sides and bring them up to your head. Gently knock on each side of your skull in a rhythmic fashion, moving the hands forwards and backwards on the skull.

Lower your hands back to your starting position.

This is the beating the heavenly drum exercise. It is useful to extend this exercise by stimulating the same areas at different levels. If you wish you can repeat this exercise, this time rubbing your hands up and down the lower back, backs of the hands facing in on the way up and palms of the hands in on the way down. Then raise your hands up to your head and massage the muscles on each side of the neck at the base of the skull, and rub the palms of your hands forwards and backwards over your scalp and face. You can repeat a third time, by placing the palms of the hands on the lower back, fingers facing down. Breathe out as if through the palms of the hands to send energy to the kidneys. Then raise your arms and guide your hands forwards and backwards over your scalp and face without actually touching the surface, just feeling the energy from your hands penetrating into your body and gently 'massaging' with the energy.

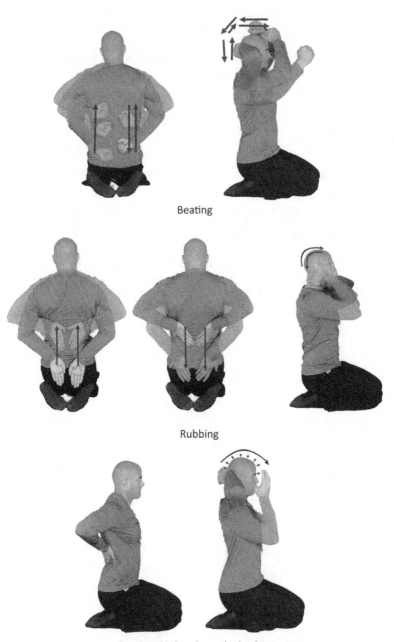

Beating

Rubbing

Resting the hands on the back,
and keeping the hands above the surface of the head and face

Mind

This exercise is a direct expression of self care. Touch is a powerful means of communication and the tissues of your body respond to your loving intention as you work through any tightness and stiffness and stimulate the energy up and down your spine.

Body

The rhythmic beating in the lower back massages the kidneys and sends vibrations up through the spinal column stimulating the nerves of the spinal cord and brain. This is then further enhanced by the physical and energy massage.

Breath

This is another exercise where the breath is not synchronised to the movement, instead just breathing freely and naturally throughout the exercise.

Chapter 7: Waking the Qi – Transition from Sitting to Standing

Having completed our sitting exercises, it is now time to rise and stand up. This sequence of exercises is designed to gently wake up the neural connections into our limbs and extend the energy into them in preparation for standing. This is particularly useful after a long sitting session, as sometimes the legs will 'go to sleep'. Instead of experiencing stiffness and soreness from suddenly requiring your legs to move and support you again, these practices gently prepare the legs for the activity of standing.

Turning the Centre

We now return our attention to our centre, known as the 'dantien' in qigong. The dantien is the physical centre of mass of our body and also the centre of our energy. In this exercise we 'turn' the energy in our dantien, a little like 'turning over' the engine of a car and warming it up before driving somewhere. This makes the energy more active and prepares it for being extended out into the limbs of our body and particularly our legs before standing.

Instructions

Sit in a comfortable position with your hands in front of your lower abdomen, one above the other and the palms facing upwards.

Tune in to any sensation of energy you have in your hands.

Raise one hand above the other and face the palm of the upper hand down so that the palms are now facing each other and it feels like there is a ball of energy between them. (Many people may not feel this ball of energy to begin with, but as you keep practicing your energy will become more active and you will be able to feel this more easily. Refer to chapter 9 for exercises that will help you to feel this energy more easily early in your practice.)

'Roll' your hands as if they were turning the ball vertically in front of your lower dantien, so that one hand replaces the other. It should feel like the poles of two magnets are changing positions.

Repeat several times.

Raise one hand and turn it over so that it faces the bottom hand

Then lower the top hand and bring the bottom hand to the top in a rolling motion. Repeat several times.

Mind

This exercise helps us to be aware of the energy in the centre of our body and the connection between the energy at our centre and in our extremities, specifically our hands.

Body

With the hands if front of our dantien, there will naturally be a connection between the energy of the hands and the energy of the dantien. Moving the hands will affect the energy in the dantien. As the polarity of the hands turn over, this stimulates the activity inside the body as well.

Breath

One common mistake people make when first beginning to focus on sensations of energy in their body is that they focus so intently that they forget to continue to breathe. In this exercise the main aim is just to keep breathing smoothly and evenly throughout it.

Extending The Legs To The Rear

In this exercise we begin to stretch and move our legs, bringing blood flow and nerve activity into them. We use our arms and eyes to help guide our awareness and energy into the limbs. We also work with the co-ordination between the upper and lower parts of the body and practice switching from same side co-ordination to opposite side co-ordination.

Same side co-ordination is easier for the body and mind to achieve, it also allows for greater bracing strength in the body. So when the body has been inactive for a long time, or very sick and weakened, or in times of very high stress, the body will often revert to this type of co-ordination.

Opposite side co-ordination is more complex and allows greater fluidity and continuity of movement. Opposite side co-ordination is usually more efficient for most types of movement but requires more complex neurological activity.

Switching from same side to opposite side co-ordination helps to bring us out of a state of neurological functioning useful for times of weakness, sickness, or high stress (such as fight or flight response), and into a state of neurological functioning which is more efficient and graceful and suitable for ongoing health and wellbeing.

Instructions

Sit in a comfortable position, with hands resting in front of the dantien.

Breathe in to prepare for the movement.

Breathe out as you extend one leg behind you, extend the arm on the same side of your body behind you as well and extend the other arm forwards. Look at the rear hand, then look at the front hand.

Breathe in crossing your arms close to your body.

Breathe out as you keep your legs in the same position and extend your opposite arm behind you and reach the other arm forwards. Look at the rear hand then look at the front hand.

Breathe in crossing your arms close to your body again.

Repeat several times.

Then as you breathe in crossing the arms, bring your extended leg back in, and on the next out breath extend the other leg behind you and repeat the exercise with this leg extended behind.

Opening on the same side

Opening on the opposite side

It is easy to adapt the exercises to sitting in a chair or on a stool

Mind

You should aim for a sense of openness and expansiveness throughout your body as you extend you limbs in different directions.

Also, as you look at each hand you are strengthening the neurological connection to each limb, as the brain recognises the visual input as matching the proprioceptive feedback it is receiving. Switching from having the arms extended on the same side as the leg to the opposite side and looking at the hands as you do this strengthens the ability to switch from same side co-ordination to opposite side co-ordination.

Body

Extending the limbs gently stretches them and allows the blood to flow into them and the nerves to become more active, quite literally filling them with energy.

Also, as you switch from having the arm on the same side of your body as the leg extended behind you to having the opposite arm extending behind you, you will feel some squeezing in your lower back in the area of the kidneys, further stimulating these in preparation for standing up.

Breath

Breathing out as you extend the limbs squeezes the muscles around the torso inwards stabilizing your core. It also encourages the flow of blood out to the limbs.

Extending The Legs To The Front

In this exercise, we switch from extending the legs behind us to extending the legs in front as further preparation for standing. This exercise gently challenges the balance and the stability of the core, and in particular the pelvic floor. Many people are surprised to find that they have a little difficulty with this movement when they first do it. This is because many people do not have good habits of engaging their pelvic floor muscles – often due to too much time spent sitting with poor posture as is common in modern society.

Instructions

Start in a sitting position with your arms crossed close in front of your body.

Breath in to prepare for the movement.

Breathe out as you rise onto your knees and extend one leg forwards. Extend the arm on the same side as the foot you have place forwards behind you, and the opposite arm forwards.

Breathe in, and return to your starting position.

Breath out, extending the other leg forward and extending the arms on the opposite side.

Breathe in and return to your starting position.

Repeat several times alternating which foot you place forward.

After completing as many repetitions on each side as you wish to, stand up by setting one foot in front of you on the ground and rising with your arms still crossed close to your body. Your legs will be much better prepared to do this now after having been extended and the energy encouraged to flow into them than it you tried to stand immediately after sitting still for a long time.

When you are standing, slowly lower your arms in front of you, giving your body time to adapt to its new standing position.

Repeat on the other side

Stand up

Mind

This exercise is very similar to the last one, except this time we go straight to opposite side co-ordination, reinforcing this type of co-ordination, and encouraging it to be our dominant habit.

Body

Many people will feel wobbly and off balance when they first do this exercise, but as you repeat the exercise you will begin to create habits of engaging the pelvic floor to stabilise your position, and this will carry over into more effective engagement of the pelvic floor and stabilisation in other postures in movements where your instability is not as obvious to you currently.

Breath

The breath in this exercise fills the same function as in the previous one, and the stabilising action of the outbreath will help with the activation of the pelvic floor as you extend one leg forwards.

Chapter 8: Waking the Qi - Standing Practices

In the Waking the Qi – Standing Practices, step by step we bring the energy from earth up though our body to connect with the energy above us through our upstretched hands. Having opened the upward flow, we then activate the downward flow back down through the body to the earth. Activating this downward flow is helpful not only for connecting and tapping in to the heavenly energy above us, but also for discharging excess or stagnant energy that may have built up in our bodies.

Rise and Fall

You will remember from the exercise in chapter two, that whenever we move part of our body, the rest of the body responds either with movement or tension to keep the forces balanced. In this exercise we will use simple movements with our arms to send a wave of energy through our body from bottom to top by channelling the force of this movement, gently stimulating every cell of the body on the way through.

Instructions

Stand comfortably with your feet shoulder width apart.

Breathe in and raise your arms to shoulder height, extended in front of your body.

Breathe out and lower your arms smoothly back to your sides.

Repeat several times.

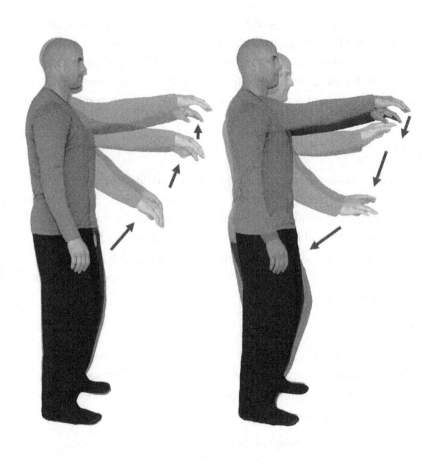

Mind

In this exercise we want to focus on the imagery of a wave moving through our body to make the transfer of forces smoother. If our body is too tense the force from the movement tends to 'skip' over parts of the body, 'jumping' from one spot to another instead of flowing smoothly through all of the tissues. By focusing on a wave sensation we can move the energy from the movement smoothly and sequentially through our whole body, starting from the feet as we move upwards and descending from the hands as we move downwards. This makes the movement more efficient and causes less wear and tear on our body.

Body

The wave of movement through our body quite literally moves and massages every cell gently on the way through. This helps to keep the cells healthy and stimulates the energy production in that cell. So as the wave of physical force moves through our body we find other types of energy moving through our body as well, such as electrical energy from the stimulation of the nerves and heat from the cellular activity and so on.

Breath

When we inhale, it is natural for our lungs to fill from the bottom upwards as the primary driver of the breath is the diaphragm which sits under the ribs. Our body also naturally expands on the inhalation. On the exhale these are reversed.

So by inhaling as we raise the arms and move the wave of energy upwards, we support the movement of energy from the arms with the natural movement caused by the breath, and we support the downward movement of energy from the arms with the exhalation of the breath. In this way the breath and body movement work in harmony together.

Bounding Leopard (Breathing Squat)

This exercise is a type of 'breathing squat' where our breath is synchronised with our movement as we perform a squatting motion. It is called 'Bounding Leopard' because if you take the movement and instead of looking at it vertically, look at it horizontally, it resembles the movement of a leopard bound across the plains.

Instead of simply rising and falling, this exercise causes the energy of the movement to circulate in a cyclical fashion up the back of the body and down the front. It is also more vigorous and engages the strength of the legs more within the movement. This extra exertion helps to further wake and activate the qi.

Instructions

Stand comfortably with your feet shoulder width apart.

Breath in as you raise your arms up high above your head and reach backwards.

Breath out, swing your arms forward and down as you bend your legs and squat so that your fingertips brush the ground.

Breath in drawing the hands upwards close to the body until they are high above your head reaching backwards again.

Repeat several times.

Some people may have difficulty squatting down low enough to brush their fingertips on the ground. As with all qigong exercises, it is important not to strain while doing them. You can still do the exercise to the best of your ability though. Even if you cannot squat at all, just moving your arms in the described pattern will stimulate the energy in the desired fashion. If you can bend your knees just a little that will help. As you continue to practice you will find that your range of motion improves little by little.

Foot placement at the bottom of the squat can be either flat footed or on the ball of the foot. These foot placements have slightly different effects, but for our purposes in this series of practices either one is fine. Some people will find one easier than the other so do whichever is more comfortable to you.

Mind

The imagery of a bounding leopard helps us to make the movement more graceful and agile, and helps us to put more energy into the movement

Body

Moving in a cyclical fashion encourages continuity of movement, the movement never stops as such it just transitions from one phase to another. This means the energy never gets stuck in one spot, it always has somewhere to move on to. In addition to this the nature of this particular cyclical action stimulates the sympathetic nervous system up the spine and parasympathetic nervous system down the front of the body sequentially. This is very healthy for the body, alternating between activation and relaxation. This is a type of stimulation of what is referred to in qigong as the 'microcosmic orbit'. We learn more about this in other practices – in particular *Between Heaven and Earth* from Long White Cloud Qigong goes into more detail on the significance of the microcosmic orbit.

Breath

This exercise can be very vigorous if you choose (depending on how quickly or slowly you do the movements) this will challenge the breathing to take full deep breaths while responding to the different compressions put on the body as the force of the movement travels through it. Developing skill in breathing through this exercise helps to make breathing easy during other vigorous activities.

Eagle Spreads It's Wings and Soars

This exercise brings the energy up into the chest and ribs. It concentrates the energy here and makes it glow brighter and more active as we gradually raise the energy higher in the body.

Instructions

Stand comfortably with your feet shoulder width apart.

Breathe in deeply as you extend your hands in front of your body, palms facing towards your body.

Hold your breath and clap your hands behind your body and then in front of your body, quickly and repeatedly. Clap as many times as is comfortable for you.

Breathe out and push your hands forwards, palms facing out, at chest level. Sink you weight downwards by bending your legs as you do this.

Repeat several times.

It is important that you only do as many claps as is comfortable to you, and also only swing your arms and clap as fast as is comfortable to you. Different people will have different capacities, and it is important to work with your capacities in order to develop them rather than comparing yourself to others.

Clap behind and in front as many times as comfortable with breath held, before breathing out and pushing forwards with your hands

Mind

During this exercise as you hold your breath you may experience some 'air hunger' as you use up the air in your lungs with the physical activity of swinging your arms and clapping your hands. This is natural and normal. It is good to experience some mild discomfort and to tune into and become more familiar with your body's needs and signals. You will find after doing this exercise several times that there is a level of exertion and amount of time holding your breath that leaves you feeling more energised after doing it than before. If you do more than this you will likely feel tired afterwards, if you do less than this the exercise will not have as noticeable an effect on you. Your capacity for this exercise will also change as you get better at it and also day to day according to what other factors may be affecting you, so the only way to hit this sweet spot consistently is by tuning into the signals from your own body.

Body

One of the main effects of this exercise is that it stretches and loosens the muscles and connective tissue around the ribs, making the ribcage more flexible. This lends itself to better general mobility, but also makes breathing using the rib muscles easier which is important for high intensity physical activity.

Breath

One interesting thing that happens during this exercise when it is done correctly at the sweet spot of exertion for you as an individual is that the whole body warms up. This actually comes as a result of the build-up of carbon dioxide in the blood and the effect this has on increasing uptake of oxygen by the cells. It is like restricting the airflow to a flame to create a draw of air through the furnace to increase the heat and size of the flame. In this way the exercise stokes the overall metabolic fire in the body. You can learn more about this in *Release the Power of Your Breath* from Long White Cloud Qigong

Dragon Spies It's Prey

This exercise raises the energy of the body up to the head and eyes and opens the awareness outwards, strongly activating the brain.

Instructions

Stand comfortably with your feet shoulder width apart.

Breath in as you raise your crossed arms in front of your body, palms facing inwards

Breathe out as your hands reach over your head and pull down and outwards to the sides of your body, making claws with the outward facing hands. Finish the out breath when your hands are level with your eyes. Follow your hands with your eyes throughout the exercise

Repeat several times.

Mind

Where we look with our eyes naturally effects our mood, focus and also the parts of our brain that we access. In this exercise as we follow our hands with our eyes as we breathe in and raise our hands with our arms crossed in front of us, our attention is naturally subdued as we look downwards to begin with, and inwards as our hands are close in front of us. As our hands reach high and then wide as we breathe out and lower our hands to the sides, our energy is naturally activated and our brain is encouraged to switch on all its parts as we attempt to see wide in all directions as we try to keep our hands in our peripheral vision.

There is a beneficial cycling between inward and subdued and then outward and active brain activity as we repeat this exercise.

Body

Pulling the arms downwards to the sides with some tension as we make claws with our hands causes the muscles of the back to activate in the pulling motion and open the shoulders wide. This encourages the neck and shoulder muscles which may have been holding the shoulders in to relax in an active way and can help to reduce tension in this area.

Breath

The downward pulling movement as the hands are lowered opens the shoulders wide while also activating the muscles of the ribcage which encourages widening of the ribs, allowing for easier sideways expansion of the ribcage resulting in easier active breathing.

Stir the Clouds

In this exercise we gently stimulate the arms, spine, and legs with a gentle swaying motion, preparing the pathways for the descending energy to come. We also continue to build energy in our upstretched hands in preparation for a downwards discharge.

Instructions

Stand comfortably with feet shoulder width apart and hands high above your head.

Sway gently side to side as if you were stirring the clouds with your hands.

Breathe deep relaxed breaths throughout.

Mind

In this exercise our attention is on the heavens above us and we focus on feeling the energy above us with our hands. As we do this we should get a sense of energy gathering and building.

Body

This exercise loosens the whole spine with gentle wave like movements side to side and in particular loosens the shoulders and helps them to move more freely.

Breath

The stimulation of this exercise builds up energy and is gentle preparation of the pathways for a sudden release in the following exercises. The deep relaxed breathing supports this gentle preparation.

Thunder

This exercise is our final preparation for the short sharp release of energy that will follow in the next exercise (Lightning). It is more vigorous than the previous exercise (Stir the Clouds) as we clear the pathways and activate them ready for the passage of energy.

Instructions

Stand comfortably with hands raised high above your head and your feet shoulder width apart.

Lift and then stamp down each foot one after the other. Breathe out a short sharp exhalation with each stamp.

Repeat several times.

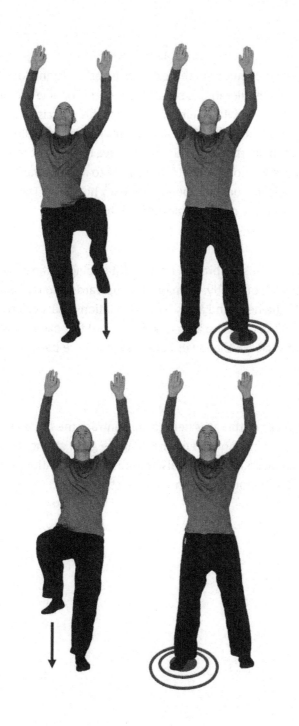

Mind

The stamping movement in this exercise is assertive and loud. Similar to the chanting earlier in this series of practices, people are often shy about making noise with their movements. This exercise should ideally be loud if at all possible, and it is disinhibiting to allow ourselves to make this noise. Sometimes we don't want to make noise because we don't want to be rude or to make someone else uncomfortable, or for other people to really notice us. This exercise helps us to become comfortable with all those things.

Body

This exercise sends a vibration from the stamping of the ground all the way up through our body, from our legs upwards into the spine and onwards to the head and arms. The stimulation is particularly strong in the lower back and the area of kidneys, and this exercise will help to loosen muscles in the lower back that may have become tight or weak.

Breath

The short sharp outbreaths help to concentrate the force and energy from this stamping movement, meaning we get a stronger stimulus from each repetition. You can also do this exercise with relaxed deep breathing throughout for a more gentle stimulation.

Lightning

In this exercise we create a rapid descent of energy by quickly lowering our hands combined with a rapid outbreath. This rapid downward descent is like lightning striking and activates the energy throughout the whole body.

Instructions

Stand comfortably with feet shoulder width apart and hands raised high above your head.

Breathe out as you lower your hands as quickly and smoothly as you can, sinking your legs as you do this.

Breathe in and raise your hands to the starting position.

Repeat several times.

Mind

Having gradually raised the energy up during the preceding exercises, this exercise represents a sudden return to earth and grounding, bringing something extra down from the heavens.

Body

The sudden fast movement in this exercise is very stimulating to the nerves. The sudden burst of nervous stimulation is very effective at clearing out disrupted nerve activation patterns – part of what contributes to what is known as 'stagnant energy' stored in the body. It also leaves the body feeling tingling and alive with fresh new vital energy.

Breath

Naturally when you are co-ordinating your breath with your movement, when you move quickly, you will also breathe quickly.

Standing in the Rain

The final exercise in the Waking the Qi series is standing in the rain. Having activated the downward flow through the 'Lightning' exercise, 'Standing in the Rain' helps to continue this downward washing and clearing of energy in a gentle way.

Instructions

Stand comfortably with feet shoulder width apart and arms relaxed by the sides.

In your mind, imagine standing with gentle rain falling all around and on you.

Pause in this position and with this mental focus for several breaths.

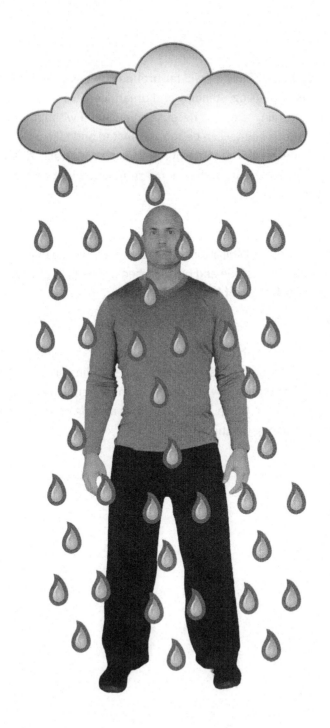

Mind

The mental focus of having rain fall around you has a significant effect on this time of pausing, standing and breathing. This step is important after the 'Lightning' exercise because if you stand without the focus of gentle rain, your energy can be too stimulated and take on a 'scorched' feel to it. The sense of rain falling counteracts this and allows you to benefit from the energy stimulation of 'Lighting' in a more gentle way.

Body

Taking time to stand still after your practice allows the energy you have stimulated to settle and be absorbed by the cells of your body so you can make full use of it.

Breath

Your breathing may have become quite active, fast and heavy during some of the qigong exercises. Pausing and standing allows your breathing to gradually slow and become more gentle as you ease your level of stimulation down and relax before moving on to other activities or qigong practices.

Chapter 9: Awareness of Energy

The exercises in the *Waking the Qi* series are designed to stimulate your energy and make it feel lively and active. Hopefully you can feel this as you go through the practices, and particularly after having done them for some time. If you are new to qigong though, you may not feel this energy strongly to begin with, and you might be curious as to what this might feel like.

This chapter will present some simple exercises to help you get a taste for feeling your energy.

Rubbing Hands
Instructions

Rub your hands quickly and firmly against each other until they become warm.

This warmth, which of course is a type of energy, is caused by the friction from the rubbing. Once warm, the cells in your hands become more active and continue to generate more energy from their cellular activity. The action of rubbing also brings your attention to the area and the neurological pathways from your brain start to become more active.

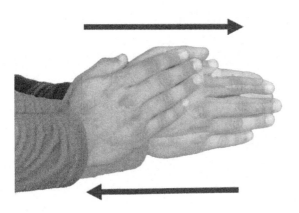

Clapping
Instructions

Clap your hands vigorously together at random intervals (no set rhythm). Clap hard enough that your hands start to tingle.

This vigorous clapping stimulates the nerve endings in your hands and makes them much more active than usual, causing the tingling.

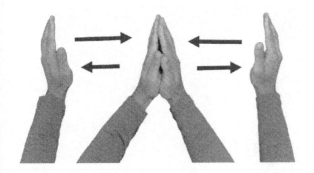

Feel the Field
Instructions

Bring your hands close together palms facing each other, maybe a couple of centimetres or an inch or so apart from each other. Pause and see if you can feel energy between your hands.

The rubbing and clapping have stimulated the activity in your nerves and all the cells in your hands, and also brought your awareness to this area. See if you can feel some of the heat from the rubbing, or magnetic field from the electrical activity in your nerves between your hands, or maybe both of these combined. You may feel other things as well.

Remember to keep breathing steadily throughout the exercise. Sometimes when we concentrate very strongly we hold our breath, but holding your breath would reduce the flow of energy to your hands in these exercises, so keep breathing.

Cycling
Instructions

Move the palms of your hands past each other in small circles. The action is a bit like if you were pedalling a bike with your hands, one moving forward as the other moves backwards. See what you can feel in the energy between your hands.

This exercise gives us a bit more of a feel for the energy between our hands as we start to feel the energy more as magnetic poles moving past each other.

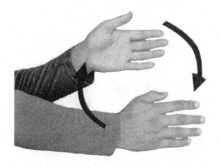

Pulling and Pushing
Instructions

With your palms close together, draw them apart a little while focusing on the sensation of energy between your hands, then squeeze back in on the energy feeling the gentle resistance from the energy field between your hands. Gradually see if you can get your hands further and further apart.

Don't try to rush this, and don't be concerned if you lose the feeling of energy as your hands get further apart. Like many other things, this is a skill that will get easier with practice.

Forming a Ball
Instructions

With the palms of your hands a comfortable distance apart so that you can still feel the energy between them, start to move the hands as if they were rubbing around the outside of a ball, feeling the energy between your hands.

You can practice making the ball of energy larger and smaller as you do this exercise.

Qi Storage
<u>Instructions</u>

After practicing these energy awareness exercises bring the palms back facing the body and squeeze them together making the ball of energy smaller until it is maybe the size of a large grapefruit or softball.

Draw the ball of energy back into your body by placing the palms of your hands on your lower abdomen underneath your belly button. Let the activated energy from the palms of your hands flow back into your body. Pause for a few moments to let your energy settle.

When we make our energy very active it is important that we take time to settle the energy afterwards and also to return the energy to our body so that it is not wasted. It takes effort and exertion for the body to generate energy in this way and if we do not settle and store the energy afterwards it is a bit like turning the heat on (or the air-conditioning depending on the season), and then leaving all the windows open. A lot of energy can be expended for no useful purpose, and this can actually be quite tiring to the body (like getting a big electricity bill). Storing the energy back in our lower dantien will mean it is available for us to use productively within our bodies.

Sensations of Energy

These exercises will have given you a start on what qi feels like when it radiates outside of your body. It may help you to have a better sense of your energy when doing some of the exercises earlier in this book such as 'Turning the Centre' in chapter 7, and some of 'Beating the Heavenly Drum' in chapter 6. As you continue to practice qigong you will find that from time to time you notice new different qualities to your energy that you have not experienced before as your energy becomes stronger.

This external radiation of energy forms a significant part of some qigong practices and becomes particularly useful when you want to start to put your energy to use such as in qigong healing, or martial arts. It is important though that before you attempt to use your external energy radiation in this way, that you have first made the energy inside your body healthy and strong, so early in your qigong practice, paying attention to the sensations of energy inside your body is more important than external radiated qi.

The sensations of energy inside your body may feel a lot like those you feel radiated externally and may include other sensations as well. Some of these sensations may include heat, numbness, tickling, tingling, vibration and more. Don't go seeking these unusual sensations, but don't be concerned if you encounter them during your practice either. If you experience any sensations that are uncomfortable or unpleasant to you and persist, seek the advice of a skilled qigong practitioner in case there may be something it is wise for you to adjust in your qigong practice.

Most importantly the sensations of energy in your body should make you feel alive! Qi means vital living energy, and we know we are doing our qigong practice right when we feel more alive and vital each time after we practice.

Chapter 10: A Wide World of Qigong to Explore

This book has included a series of qigong exercises designed to wake up your qi and make it more lively and active. This is an excellent place to start in your qigong practice, and begin to make your qi healthier and stronger. After practicing the exercises in this book for some time, you may wish to explore the world of qigong further by learning and practicing other sets of qigong exercises.

Within the world of qigong there are many such sets of qigong exercises, each focusing on different things. Long White Cloud Qigong offers books, dvds, online courses, and other resources for learning a range of these practices that you might like to consider.

Below are some of the practices Long White Cloud Qigong has to offer:

Twelve Rivers Qigong

This is a set of twelve qigong exercises that stimulate the organ meridians in the body. These meridians are the same meridians as those used in acupuncture and are like rivers of energy that flow through our bodies. Twelve Rivers Qigong gives us a practical understanding of these meridians and how organ function, posture and emotion affect each other. Practicing Twelve Rivers Qigong activates the meridians, corrects posture, balances emotions and helps to keep our organs healthy and strong.

Between Heaven and Earth

This practice works with the extraordinary meridians in the body. The energy flows in these meridians are powerful like ocean currents. These meridians relate more to the muscles, connective tissue, bones, and nerves in our bodies. Working with these meridians helps us to understand another layer of our energetic functioning, and when they are fully active allow us to connect more strongly to the energy of heaven and energy of earth.

Enter the Flow

The aim of the Enter the Flow practices is to develop habits of movement and awareness that allow our energy to move freely throughout our bodies like rain, refreshing and renewing every cell of our body with every movement. Through the Enter the Flow course your every movement can become a kind of moving meditation and qigong practice.

Qigong Meditation

Qigong Meditation teaches a series of meditations that take you step by step to an amazing place of clarity and stillness. Many people say that these meditations have changed their lives.

Movement in Stillness

Zhan Zhuang or Standing Post is a very powerful type of qigong practice where by standing in stillness externally we find that the energy moves more freely and powerfully inside. Movement in Stillness teaches a selection of these powerful practices and includes instruction on how to get the most out of these practices by avoiding common mistakes.

Qigong Walking

Walking is something that most of us do regularly as part of our daily lives. By walking with qigong awareness you can learn to walk in a way that causes less wear and tear on your body and stimulates your energy flow. Qigong walking teaches a series of walking practices that help you to maintain healthy energy flow and a full and vibrant energy field throughout your day.

Introduction to Qigong Healing

When our own energy is healthy and strong, we are able to use this energy to help others. Introduction to Qigong Healing provides an introduction to using your energy in this way. It is best to have developed a firm foundation in your own qigong practice before exploring this area of qigong application.

Wild Animal Play

Some of the earliest qigong practices involved mimicking the movements of different animals and feeling what these do to the energy of your body. Wild Animal Play teaches movements from Tiger, Snake, Crane, Leopard, and Dragon qigong. These movements are vigorous and great for developing strength, flexibility, balance, agility, power, and fluidity of movement. Underlying theory and relationships to the five elements are also taught for each of these practices.

Release the Power of Your Breath

Breathing is at the centre of qigong, and at the centre of life. Release the Power of Your Breath gives a foundational understanding of the breathing function including anatomy, physiology, chemistry, and psychology. It then applies this understanding to relaxation, alertness, physical performance, and energy awareness.

Further Resources

You can find information about each of these including many free videos on the Long White Cloud Qigong website at
http://www.longwhitecloudqigong.com

Chapter 11: FAQs

As many people have never heard of qigong before, I often get the same questions from different people when they are first exposed to it. Or if they have heard of qigong, there are some common misconceptions out there that they may have come across that they ask me about.

For your interest I have included this section on answers to frequently asked questions about qigong to satisfy your curiosity and to clarify a few things you may have heard about in relation to qigong.

In the interests of space, I will keep the answers here concise, but many of these questions could well justify a full essay to answer in detail. If you are interested to learn more about any of these topics, you might want to check out the News & Articles section of the Long White Cloud Qigong website, as from time to time I do write longer pieces on topics of interest and post them there.

Isn't Qigong just for old people?

It is true that lots of older people do qigong for the benefits that it gives them in staying healthy, reducing aches and pains, and improving general wellbeing, but this does not mean that qigong is only for old people. Young people can benefit just as much. For them it is more about performance optimization and building a foundation of health for the future. We see this most prominently in the martial arts where normal physical training only takes you so far and to go further you need to understand and practice using the more subtle understanding that qigong imparts. Anyone seeking peak performance will benefit from qigong training, whether that be in sport, business, creativity, or any aspect of life.

Qigong Is 'Internal', it works only on the energy. It can't give you a beautiful body like other types of exercise can it?

I saw this idea expressed in an article on qigong in the New York Times once. What a load of nonsense! The beauty and health of our physical body flows from the health of our internal energy. I think the idea that qigong somehow only works on the energy and not the physical body comes from people taking a mystical approach to qigong, and as a result 'imagining' they are doing qigong without ever developing any real skill with their energy and connecting that through to their physical bodies. Of course the beauty of your physical body should not be the primary criteria for judging the success of your qigong practice (or any type of exercise for that matter), but as you get healthier and happier your body tends to look better as well.

What is the difference between Qigong and Taiji (also spelt Tai Chi)?

Qigong is a broad concept that incorporates all practices and methods for developing skill with energy. Taiji is a martial art that uses certain aspects of qigong as part of the training process. As such Taiji is a subset of qigong. Practicing Taiji is excellent for health particularly focusing on balance, co-ordination, and circulation, which is why so many people now practice it for this purpose rather than focusing on it as a martial art. However, all the movements are still martial/fighting movements. Within the broader scope of qigong most practices are not martial in nature and this means that they are focused more specifically on other purposes. For example, a movement that is excellent for strengthening one of your organs such as your bladder or your stomach may have no martial purpose, therefore you would not find it in Taiji, but you would find it within other qigong practices.

What is the difference between Qigong and Yoga?

Qigong and Yoga are different cultural expressions of the same deeper truth, that our minds and bodies are linked together and we can influence them through mindful physical practice. When we become skilled at this we have greater awareness of the living energy that flows through us, called 'qi' in qigong and 'prana' in yoga. There are analogous practices throughout qigong and yoga. Still and moving postures, breathing techniques, meditation, dietary advice and so on.

The differences are more about flavour and expression. I like to compare the different practices to Chinese food and Indian food, they taste quite different to each other, but if you dig down they are both about nutrition and making you healthy. Some people like Chinese food, other people like Indian food, some people like both. Each of them can be very good for you when prepared with skill and understanding. Some of the typical differences in 'flavour' between them is that qigong tends to emphasize practice standing up where yoga tends to emphasize practice sitting, lying and in other postures down on the ground. Qigong practice tends to emphasize flowing movements, whereas yoga practice tends to emphasize still postures.

Are there any restrictions on doing Qigong?

Most qigong practices are very safe and can be practiced by anyone, however if you have significant health issues or injuries you will need to consult with a health practitioner or experienced instructor to understand if there are some practices you should avoid or may need to modify to avoid aggravating an existing condition. In addition to this there are some practices that should not be attempted until you have developed your energy and gained enough experience through other practices. These practices are generally classified as 'advanced', and should always come with appropriate warnings if they are taught by a responsible instructor. One general restriction on qigong practice is that anyone with a psychotic disorder should not practice qigong, unless they do so under psychiatric supervision.

Why is Qigong so slow?

This is a common misconception about qigong. Qigong is not always done slowly, and in fact some exercises specifically require fast movement (such as the 'Lightning' exercise in this book). However, qigong should always be done unrushed and with great awareness to develop skill. To begin with this usually means doing the practices very slowly to allow time to perceive every detail of what is going on. Later as skill develops, this same level of awareness can be maintained at greater speeds.

130

Throughout the different Long White Cloud Qigong practices you are encouraged to try doing qigong exercises both slow and fast. You will find that you gain different benefits from doing the practices at different speeds, and as you gain more experience you will be able to change the speed of your practice according to how you are feeling and what you need at a given time.

Is Qigong some kind of martial art?

The short answer is no, qigong is not a martial art. Qigong is anything that develops skill with energy, and historically this has been applied to many martial arts, most obviously Taiji, but also many forms of kung fu, and even martial arts from other cultures use qigong principles to achieve peak performance. But qigong can and is often focused on other things which are not specifically martial arts. Health and wellbeing is the most common application of qigong practice.

Is Qigong Chinese?

The short answer is yes, qigong comes from China and the word 'qigong' is Chinese. But is qigong really Chinese? If we dig deeper in our understanding we see that qigong is universal, its principles apply to all of us regardless of our cultural background. We do qigong and ourselves a great disservice if we tie it down to one cultural origin when the principles of qigong can actually be found at least in part through the practices of many cultures and also of course in nature itself.

We don't think of ourselves as engaging in a Greek cultural practice when we are doing geometry, even though the Greeks contributed greatly to our understanding of it. We are just doing something that works... And more importantly, while we look back and learn from the early innovations in geometry, we also look forward and continue to research to gain more and better understanding.

The same is true of qigong. It is something that works. When we cloak it too strongly in cultural interpretation we can miss the actual principles that are important. We can also tend to look backwards trying to replicate the past, rather than learn from the past and look forward with curiosity to the future.

I have seen two different people do the same Qigong exercise differently from one another. Is one right and the other wrong?

There are many reasons why two people may do the same exercise differently. One may have adapted the exercise to better suit their physical needs or limitations while still preserving the original purpose of the exercise, but still making it look quite different. Alternatively, one may have decided to emphasize certain principles in the exercise more or less to change its purpose to better suit what they are wanting to work on, thus resulting in an exercise that looks almost the same but has quite a different effect. Both of these are 'right', they are thoughtful adaptations of the exercise.

On the other hand, one might be doing the exercise differently because they can't remember it properly, or they might have tried adapting the exercise but done so in a way that doesn't achieve the purpose they desire or is in fact harmful to them. That would be 'wrong'.

'Right' or 'Wrong' in qigong cannot be determined by whether an exercise looks the same as someone else's version of the exercise, but rather by whether it achieves its purpose satisfactorily.

How many styles of Qigong are there?

There are literally THOUSANDS of styles of qigong. A lot of this is due to the process of adaptation described in the answer to the previous question, carried out by many people over many years. This diversity of practice is wonderful and means that you are sure to be able to find a style that achieves the purposes you seek and suits your preferences. It also means that there is so much variety that you will never get bored. To go back to a food analogy, it means there are lots and lots of different dishes for you to try. Of course within this variety you will probably come up with a few favourites that you enjoy and practice most of the time, but there will always be something new for you to try when you feel like trying something different.

If there are so many styles of qigong, how can I find what is right for me?

The best answer is to go and try a few. Use your senses. Does it look like something that you would enjoy? How does it make you feel when you do it? If you enjoy it and it makes you feel good, you are probably on the right track. After trying a few different types of practice you will begin to get a better understanding of the differences between practices and of what appeals to you. If you have specific goals you wish to achieve it may also be useful to ask someone who has experience with a lot of styles already, as they may be able to point you to what you seek more quickly than by trying out each style yourself.

What is Qi?

Plain and simply 'qi' is energy in all its many forms. Electricity, magnetism, heat, light, vibration, tension, momentum, chemical and more. What makes 'qi' special is that when we talk about 'qi' we are usually talking about 'living energy'. This means that it is directed by an intelligence. It doesn't respond purely mechanically, but instead responds intelligently. This makes working with it fascinating as often it will respond better to being persuaded than it will to being forced, and has limitless rather than limited potential.

Is Qigong a type of Religion (or superstition)?

As we work with 'qi' we gain a better understanding of ourselves and our place in the universe. Historically some people have extrapolated this out and turned this into a religious or superstitious belief. This can be limiting as once something becomes religious or superstitious it often becomes dogmatic, and things are 'believed' because of this dogma, regardless of what is actually experienced. This can close the mind to new experience and learning and understanding more. I think it is more beneficial to keep your mind open and curious to learn and understand. Practicing qigong does not need to be any more religious or superstitious than studying say physics or chemistry. Each can open our mind to a greater understanding of the wonders of life and the universe, and our further progress in each is held back if we become dogmatic in our beliefs rather than open and curious.

Is Qigong Dangerous?

In general no, qigong is not dangerous and can be practiced by just about anyone without restriction. Common sense should always prevail though. Even something as safe as say going for a walk, which is a healthy activity for almost everyone, will not be suitable for some people due to existing injury or illness. So there may be reasons why qigong would not be good for certain individuals, but these are the rare exception.

One way that qigong can become dangerous is when people practice one type of exercise excessively or too intensively. Again, comparing this to going for a walk, this would be like someone continuing to walk long after they have developed blisters on their feet and then turning those into sores... and so on, because they think it has to be good for them and nothing bad could ever come from walking... Common sense is the only precaution most people need to take in their qigong practice.

Can Qigong give me super powers?

Practice of qigong can lead to the development of skills that a lot of people would consider unusual. Extraordinary physical resilience and the ability to generate and channel energy for healing purposes being some of the most common of these. Of course these are not superpowers, but ordinary abilities that most people have not developed, or at least not to a high degree. Someone who has these skills is no different from someone who is extraordinarily strong and can lift heavy things, or can jump really high, or perhaps someone who can play beautiful music. It is the result of a lot of focused practice, maybe combined with some natural talent.

To begin with though it is better to focus simply on developing your own health rather than developing some extraordinary skill, as whatever skill you wish to develop will be compromised and limited if it is not built on a foundation of health and wellbeing.

What science is there to support the effectiveness of Qigong?
There has been research done on various aspects of qigong and how it helps with different health conditions. There are quite a few small-scale studies showing specific benefits in a number of areas. A bit of googling, or searching through relevant academic journal databases will show up quite a bit of scientific research in this area, but overall this is an emerging field with a lot more research to be done to better understand the mechanisms through which qigong practice works and its effectiveness in its many applications.

Why haven't I heard of Qigong before?
While qigong has been massively popular in Asia for a long time, it is only now starting to become popular in the West as people discover for themselves the health and wellbeing they can achieve from regular practice. Awareness in the West has grown massively in the last couple of decades, but still has a long way to go yet. It is growing though, and you hearing about qigong now is evidence of that.

Why don't more hospitals and medical clinics use qigong if it is so effective?
Mainly because awareness of qigong is only now emerging in the West. In China there are several hospitals that specialize in using qigong to treat a variety of illnesses. In the West this is less common, but if you search you may be able to find skilled qigong therapists working in private practice, and there are some hospitals that have programs which use qigong to assist with post-operative recovery and recovery after other treatments as they have found this to be a very cost effective way to speed up the healing process. Hopefully as more research on the efficacy of qigong is done and awareness grows,

qigong will become available more readily in hospitals and medical clinics.

If I do Qigong I don't need to go to the doctor, right?

Qigong can certainly help you to maintain your health and even recover from many conditions and illnesses. But there are many things that you may still need additional medical assistance with, so it is wise to maintain your relationship with your doctors, even though you may find that you do not need to visit them as often.

Can Qigong make me immortal?

The quest for immortality has long been the stuff of myth and legend in cultures all over the world. China is no exception, and some of these legends sprang up around qigong practice. Qigong can certainly help you to live a longer and healthier life, but the nature of this existence is that death is also part of life. Qigong can help us to understand and accept this and to live our lives more fully and joyfully.

I have heard that Qigong includes sexual practices, is this true?

It stands to reason that the creation of new life utilizes some of the most powerful energy or 'qi' we experience in this life. For this reason, research into the use of this powerful energy has been an area of interest for some qigong practitioners. Using such a powerful energy can lead to powerful results, but with great power also comes greater potential for harm. As such all qigong sexual practices should be considered 'advanced' practices and should not be engaged in without the advice of a suitably experienced qigong teacher.

Also it is important to consider your motivation in exploring this area, and the qigong teacher's motivation in teaching it. Unfortunately, as with every other field of expertise, qigong expertise is not always applied for the purest purposes. Some unscrupulous individuals will seize upon any opportunity to enhance their own power and achieve their own gratification. If any sexual practice falls outside your own personal morality, or if you have any reservations about an

136

instructor's motivation in sharing sexual practices with you, then you are better to stay away from them. There are plenty of non-sexual qigong practices capable of developing your health and vitality without needing to engage in the sexual practices.

Does attaining mastery in qigong equate to a higher level of morality?

Practice of qigong leads to many insights about yourself and the universe and how life works. Often when people gain these insights, they reflect this in their behaviour as their deepest desire is a more harmonious world. This leads some to associate qigong skill with virtue or morality, especially as historically many highly skilled qigong practitioners were monks whose express purpose was the relief of suffering.

Unfortunately skill and morality are not always associated. Knowledge does not always lead to wisdom, and there are corrupt monks as well as good ones, just as there are people with good and bad intentions and motivations in any field. If your intentions are pure, then practicing qigong will help you along your way to a greater understanding and ability to live morally, but not everyone chooses this path. So it is important to judge each person you encounter on their merits and not assume that their skill in one area necessarily means that they have other characteristics.

I have heard that Qigong will take a lifetime to learn?

Learning qigong is really not that different from learning other skills. Some people will learn faster than others, and some people will have natural talents that help them to attain a higher level of skill than others over time. When people say that qigong will take a lifetime to learn, I think it can be interpreted in more than one way. Of course you can keep learning from qigong for your entire lifetime, refining your skills and gaining further insight, but you can often pick up the basics very quickly. I think sometimes when people say that something will take an entire lifetime to learn it means that they don't actually know how to learn what they are trying to achieve, and it keeps it off in the distance as a forever unattainable objective. It justifies never gaining the skill. There is a big difference between something taking a lifetime to learn, and something continuing to be refined over a lifetime.

Is Qigong an ancient art?

Well yes and no. Qigong certainly has ancient roots as people long ago discovered relationships between mind, body and energy, and developed practices for working with them. But if we think of qigong as an ancient art, we may think that the ultimate aim is to replicate it as it was practiced anciently. This can lead to the idea that we can never be as good as 'the ancients'. Of course we will never fully replicate the ancients, because we live in a different time with a different environment and different experiences to inform our understanding and practice. Qigong is about life and vitality, as such is should be adapted to our times to help us to gain the most life and vitality from our current situation and continue to change as our environment and lives change. So qigong at its best is a LIVING ART, it has ancient roots, a modern current expression, and openness and curiosity about the future.

Where did qigong come from?

Qigong emerged from observation and experience with nature. The exact origins of some of what we now refer to as qigong is lost in the mists of time, but there are stories that make sense though. One such story is that many thousands of years ago in ancient China, the workers would come back from the fields at night and be cold and damp. They found that by dancing and making movements that mimicked animals they were able to avoid aches, pains and illnesses caused by these living conditions. Over time their understanding became more refined and they began to understand how different movements and imagery had different effects on their bodies and health. Little by little a more sophisticated understanding of mind, body, health and movement developed.

I've heard people talk about 'lineage' when discussing qigong and martial arts. What are they talking about, and is this important?

Lineage refers to who taught you the style that you practice, and who taught them, and who taught them, and so on. It is similar to the idea of heredity, like an art can be 'inherited'. There was a lot of truth to this in the past because most teaching was kept secret, and often within a family or temple. As such being taught at all, and certainly any 'deeper' secrets, was a kind of inheritance, and 'lineage' was highly relevant in understanding the source and nature of someone's skills.

However we now live in more open times when the arts are taught more openly, and in addition it is common for people to have multiple teachers that they have sourced their knowledge from. This is a healthy development, as in the past being limited to one teacher limited your knowledge as well. Because you were usually unable to compare information with other sources you were often doomed to copy and repeat the incorrect or ineffective from your teacher as well as the useful. In our modern times most of us have moved past the idea that leadership should be passed on as a hereditary right, preferring instead that leaders be chosen based on merit. Similar with the idea of lineage in qigong and the martial arts, most often it is a distraction, having learned from a particular person is no guarantee that skill has actually been developed or understanding acquired. While discussion of lineage sometimes uncovers interesting history, for current practice it is far better to focus on individual merit.

What is the relationship between Qigong and creativity?

Qigong has long been known to enhance creativity, developing awareness of subtlety in our self and coming to understand the connection between things in our experience of the world opens us up to new opportunities and ways of seeing things. In addition to this, physiologically qigong practice leads to stronger and healthier neural pathways and increased oxygen supply to the brain which helps with optimal functioning and creativity as well.

As such, many musicians, artists, dancers, and others in creative fields find that regular qigong practice acts as an inspiration and supports them in their creative endeavours. Also, people who don't have a history of creative pursuits often find that they naturally become more interested in them after practicing qigong for a while.

This enhanced creativity will help you to gain insights about your qigong practice as well. A living qigong practice should be constantly evolving and changing as you change and develop. Long White Cloud Qigong aims to teach you the underlying principles of qigong clearly enough that you can change and adapt your qigong practice with confidence according to your evolving understanding.

Is there such a thing as too much qigong?
More is not always better. I like the analogy of growing a plant. More water will not always make it healthier, neither will more sun. A plant will need different amounts of water and sunlight at different stages of its growth, but too much water will flood its roots and loosen the soil and too much sun may scorch the leaves and dry the plant out – particularly when it is very young and just getting established. It is important to give the young plant enough, but not more than it can handle. A good way to gauge this with your qigong is to assess how you feel at the end of a session. Sometimes you may feel a little tired if you have worked hard in a session, but overall you should feel better after your session than you did before.

If I do qigong do I still need to do other types of exercise?
Qigong can do many wonderful things for you and can play a big part in keeping you healthy, fit and strong. But unless you are convalescing from a serious illness, in which case gentle qigong exercise may be your only physical activity, you will probably want to practice qigong along with other types of exercise and activity rather than having it replace them entirely. At the very least most people should be walking

regularly, as this rhythmic exercise has an important role in maintaining the health of the postural muscles and encouraging healthy blood circulation and muscle tone. And of course people may also want to engage in other types of exercise and sports that they enjoy or help them achieve their particular desires. The good thing is, that as your understanding and practice of qigong develops, you can turn every kind of activity into a type of qigong practice, whether it be by turning your regular walk into a 'Qigong Walk' by using the practices in *Qigong* Walking from Long White Cloud Qigong, or by applying the principles found in *Enter the Flow* to bring energy awareness into every movement and activity.

What is the message of qigong?

I got asked this exact question by a reporter awhile back, but it also reflects a common misconception that many people have, that qigong has a particular ideology attached to it. Qigong is a set of skills and practices that help you to understand your own functioning and your interaction with the world around you. There are many lessons to be learned from this and understanding to be gained, but no message as such, other than 'this is how the world is', how you choose to use that understanding is entirely up to you and will be determined by your own motivations and character.

Can qigong cure my...?

Qigong can be a valuable part of health maintenance and recovery from illness. But as to whether qigong can cure a specific condition, the answer is that it depends on many factors. Qigong has the potential to 'cure' i.e. help recover from almost any condition in the same way that other health building changes such as a change of diet could potentially 'cure' it. But whether it WILL 'cure' a particular condition depends very much on the severity and progression of the condition and also what the causative factors are. The best results usually come from making use of all available methods for building health and healing, one of which may be qigong working alongside other methods. As always, common sense should prevail.

Is there some kind of special diet for qigong?

I get asked this one a lot. It is not so much that there is a prescribed diet for qigong, but from qigong we can learn principles that apply to nutrition and its effects on our bodies. How we apply these principles will depend on what our aims are, but certainly qigong principles can help us to understand what and how we should eat to achieve those aims. There will be information on this topic available from Long White Cloud Qigong in the future.

About the author

Throughout his life John Munro has had an active interest in health and wellbeing. His mother was a naturopath, so throughout his early formative years he was exposed to many different natural methods for improving health and correcting illness. One of these was Qigong, and this combination of working with the mind and the body together to become aware of and direct energy fascinated him.

John went on to formally study many different aspects of health maintenance himself, gaining qualifications in Traditional Chinese Medicine, Neuro Linguistic Programming, Massage, Chinese Reflexology, Personal Training, and of course Qigong. In addition to this he has also studied physics, chemistry and philosophy at a university level. These diverse areas of study all feed into a broad practical understanding of Qigong and an ability to translate important qigong concepts into modern language.

John has previously served as the Secretary and Registrar of *The New Zealand Qigong and Traditional Chinese Medicine Association*, and as Chairperson of *Natural Health Practitioners of New Zealand*. He is also the founder of Long White Cloud Qigong, an international qigong school with students and teachers all over the world, and the author of several popular books on qigong.